CULTIVATING YOUR DREAMS INTO REALITY

VINAY RAJAGOPAL IYER

BLUEROSE PUBLISHERS
India | U.K.

Copyright © Vinay Rajagopal Iyer 2024

All rights reserved by author. No part of this publication may be reproduced, stored in a retrieval system or transmitted in any form or by any means, electronic, mechanical, photocopying, recording or otherwise, without the prior permission of the author. Although every precaution has been taken to verify the accuracy of the information contained herein, the publisher assumes no responsibility for any errors or omissions. No liability is assumed for damages that may result from the use of information contained within.

BlueRose Publishers takes no responsibility for any damages, losses, or liabilities that may arise from the use or misuse of the information, products, or services provided in this publication.

For permissions requests or inquiries regarding this publication, please contact:

BLUEROSE PUBLISHERS
www.BlueRoseONE.com
info@bluerosepublishers.com
+91 8882 898 898
+4407342408967

ISBN: 978-93-5989-230-6

Cover design: Rishav Rai
Typesetting: Rohit

First Edition: March 2024

Acknowledgments

Gratitude to My Remarkable Supporters

I want to say a big thank you to those who've been my rock through everything:

To Ajji and Doddappa,

You've been my guardians, teaching me about love, resilience, and strength. Ajji, your stories and warmth have shaped me in ways I can't describe. Doddappa, your guidance and perseverance have been my guiding light, shaping my dreams and values.

To my father, AR Rajagopala Krishnan,

You've been both mom and dad, filling our home with love and sacrifice. Your kindness and resilience have taught me so much, and your sacrifices for me are imprinted in my heart. Your love has been my stronghold, shaping who I am.

To Ritu and Aryan,

Ritu, my partner, your support and love mean everything to me. You're the heartbeat of our home, my constant through every high and low.

Aryan, my son, you've changed my view of the world. Your creativity and fresh perspective inspire me every day, reminding me of the joy and potential in seeing the world through your eyes.

To Uncle Ashok,

Your artistic genius and mentorship have added depth and beauty to my work and life. I'm so grateful for your guidance and the creativity you bring to everything you touch.

Mentors and Inspirations,

I'm grateful to visionaries like A.P.J. Abdul Kalam and Ratan Tata, and spiritual guides like Swami Vivekananda and Mahatma Gandhi, who've shaped my ethical and inspirational compass.

Thank you all for being my stars, guiding me with your light.

With all my heart,

Vinay Rajagopal Iyer

About the Author

Blending a rich technical expertise with a passion for holistic wellness, our author emerges as a multifaceted leader and visionary in both the technological and personal development arenas. With a robust educational foundation, including an MBA from the University of Melbourne and a BE in Electrical & Electronics from RV College of Engineering, the journey unfolds through various roles in technology and leadership.

The narrative begins with over two decades of global experience in technology, where our author excels as a Technology Executive. From hands-on technical roles to leadership positions, the expertise spans across infrastructure technologies, large-scale team management, and strategic oversight in international settings. Key roles include a Practice Director at Happiest Minds Technologies, a Senior Manager and Senior Consulting Architect at IBM, and a Program Manager at Apara Global Services, showcasing a trajectory marked by growth and diversification.

As the Chief Operating Officer of iSmart, the author's entrepreneurial acumen shines. Here, within a mere three months, the transformation of a startup into a thriving enterprise with an ever-expanding team is a testament to strategic brilliance and leadership prowess.

Beyond technology, our author delves into the realms of personal development and wellness. A Master Spirit Life Coach certified by the International Coaching Federation, a Strengths Coach, and a Louise Hay - Heal Your Life trainer reflect a deep commitment to empowering others. This is further enriched by certifications in Yoga, embodying a holistic approach to wellbeing.

In professional certifications, the author's dedication to continuous learning is evident. With accreditations ranging from PMI's Project Management Professional to ITIL, and technical certifications from NetApp, VMWare, and Symantec, the commitment to staying at the forefront of technological advancements is clear.

This unique blend of technical acumen, leadership, and personal development expertise makes our author a distinguished figure, guiding others through transformational journeys in both their professional and personal lives.

Pioneering Thinking: Unleashing the Power of the Mind

In the rich heritage of Indian philosophy, the practice of willpower holds a significant place, resonating deeply with the teachings of ancient scriptures. "Pioneering Thinking" is an exploration of this profound concept, drawing upon the timeless wisdom of the Upanishads and the modern advances in psychology and personal development.

The book delves into the art of using one's imagination to manifest desires and achieve goals. It is a journey that transcends mere wishful thinking, evolving into an active co-creation with the cosmic energies. The narrative weaves through tales from Indian folklore and real-life stories, demonstrating how willpower has been effectively utilized in various aspects of life, from meditation to the attainment of professional success.

At its core, "Pioneering Thinking" is about understanding and harnessing the mind's latent power. It offers practical guidance on training the mind to focus, envision, and materialize thoughts into reality. The book is a guide to transcending the limitations of the physical world and tapping into a more profound source of knowledge and power.

This exploration is not just about personal achievements but also encompasses a larger vision of societal well-being. It teaches how to shape thoughts constructively and use the power of willpower to bring about positive change in the community and beyond.

For those seeking to deepen their practice, "Pioneering Thinking" references texts like "The Yoga Sutras of Patanjali," interpreted by renowned scholars, providing a comprehensive understanding of the mind's capabilities. This reference serves as a bridge connecting the ancient spiritual traditions of India with contemporary methods of personal development, presenting willpower as a powerful tool for transformation.

An Ode to the Seekers: Sharing the Journey of Willpower

Dear Companions on the Path,

In the spirit of sharing and learning, I've penned this book as a vessel to convey the remarkable insights that have profoundly enriched my life. My journey, much like the explorations of ancient Indian sages, has been a quest to unearth deeper joys and expand my horizons of understanding.

I am but a fellow traveler in the realm of Pioneering Thinking, continuously learning and discovering its boundless potential. It's a field as limitless as our imagination, offering endless possibilities for growth and creativity.

This book is crafted as a primer and a practical guide for those eager to explore and harness the power of Pioneering Thinking. The wisdom encapsulated here is not of my sole creation but a compilation of valuable insights and techniques gleaned from my explorations. It's a synthesis of diverse practices that have stood the test of time and personal experience.

In the spirit of the Upanishads, which emphasize the sharing of knowledge, I have included a list of resources at the end of this book. These sources have been my guides and mentors on this journey and may serve as beacons for you as well.

The book unfolds a variety of techniques for Pioneering Thinking. I recommend a gradual approach, akin to savoring a cup of chai, allowing each sip to reveal its layers of flavor. You may choose to journey through the book slowly, experimenting with the exercises as you go, or perhaps read it in its entirety first and then revisit it for a deeper dive.

This book is my offering to you, crafted with love and the hope that it will be a blessing in your life. May it help in nurturing the radiant light within you, bringing forth more joy, fulfillment, and beauty into your world.

With warm regards and best wishes on your journey,

Vinay

Contents

Part 1

The Dreams: Unveiling the Power of Willpower 1

Dear Comrades in the Quest for Fulfillment 1

Unveiling the Power of Imagination: The Essence
of Pioneering Thinking... 3

Manifesting Dreams: The Art of Willpower.................... 4

The Essence of Tranquility in Willpower........................ 6

Exploring the Landscape of Willpower: A Journey Within. 7

The Art of Manifesting Dreams: A Step-by-Step Guide . 9

Harnessing Willpower for Universal Good 11

Manifesting Dreams: A Guide to Positive Empowerments 12

The Art of Crafting Empowerments: Guidelines for
Positive Manifestation.. 14

Manifesting Intentions: Overcoming Doubts with
Empowerments... 16

Embracing the Spiritual Paradox: Balancing Desire
and Detachment.. 18

Navigating Life's River: The Journey of Self-
Empowerment and Willpower... 19

Part 2

**Unlocking the Power Within: The Art of
Pioneering Thinking.. 21**

The Practice Unveiled: Pioneering Thinking as a
Spiritual Tool.. 22

Embracing Universal Abundance: The Law of
Seeking and Receiving 23
Integrating Pioneering Thinking into Everyday Life 24
Incorporating Pioneering Thinking into Your Life 26
The Essence of Essence, Action, and Possession
in Life's Journey 28
Harmonizing Desire, Belief, and Acceptance: Key
Pillars of Pioneering Thinking 29
Tapping Into the Wisdom of Your Inner Self 31
Embracing Your Inner Spiritual Essence through
Meditation 32
Embracing Life's Journey with Flexibility and Trust:
An Indian Philosophical Perspective 34
Navigating Life's Journey with Intuition and Self-
Discovery: A Reflection from Indian Wisdom 36
Cultivating a Mindset of Abundance: Insights from
Indian Philosophy 38
Embracing Abundance in the Contemporary World:
An Indian Perspective 40
Willpower of Plentiful Harmony: A Guided Journey
Through India's Essence 42
Empowerments for Prosperity Rooted in Indian Ethos . 43
Embracing Your Divine Essence: A Journey to
Self-Acceptance 44
Embracing Self-Love Through Empowerments
and Willpower 46
Fostering Self-Esteem and Embracing Universal
Abundance through Willpower and Empowerments 47
Cultivating Self-Love and Recognition: A Guided
Willpower and Empowerments 49
Additional Resources: 51
Cultivating Generosity: Embracing the Flow of
Life's Energy 52

Embracing the Joy of Generosity: The Essence of
Sharing in Indian Philosophy 54

Embracing the Flow of Generosity: Cultivating the
Art of Giving in the Indian Ethos 56

Harnessing the Power of Mind for Holistic Healing:
Integrating Pioneering Thinking in Indian Wellness
Practices 58

Embracing Wholeness: Understanding the Holistic
Message of Illness in the Indian Context 61

Inner Healing: Embracing the Indian Ethos of Wellness .. 63

Inner Transformation: Tales of Healing and Wholeness
from the Heart of India 65

The Art of Distant Healing: Bridging Mind, Body,
and Spirit 67

Part 3

The Essence of Inner Harmony: Meditations and Empowerments 70

Your Words Shape Your Destiny: Wisdom from the Ages 72

Harmonizing Energy: A Meditation Inspired by
Indian Wisdom 74

Revitalizing Pranic Meditation: An Indian-Inspired
Energy Center Activation 76

Pranic Energy Circulation: An Indian-Inspired
Vitalizing Meditation 78

Crafting Your Inner Haven: An Indian-Inspired
Willpower for Serenity and Strength 80

Communing with Your Inner Sage: An Indian-
Inspired Guided Meditation 82

Encountering Your Inner Mentor: An Indian-Inspired
Meditative Practice 83

Manifesting with the Heart's Hue: An Indian-
Inspired Willpower Practice 85

Invigorating Wholeness: An Indian-Inspired Guide to Healing Meditation 87
Empowerments for Holistic Well-being: An Indian-Inspired Self-Care Mantra 88
Guidance for Energetic Healing from an Indian Cultural Perspective 90
Group Healing: An Indian Spiritual Perspective 92
Healing Through Color Willpower: A Meditative Approach for Alleviating Pain 94
Invoking Inner Qualities: An Indian-Inspired Meditative Approach 96
Empowering Empowerments: Manifesting Positivity and Transformation... 98
Empowering Empowerments in Relationships: Building Bonds of Positivity 99
Harmonious Melodies: Singing and Chanting for Transformation 101

Part 4
Advanced Methods: Mastering Manifestation Techniques 105
Discovering the Divine Essence Within: A Path to Right Relations 105
The Pioneering Thinking Journal: A Canvas of Manifestation... 107
Overcoming Inner Obstacles: A Journey of Self-Discovery 109
Unlocking Inner Barriers: A Journey to Self-Realization.. 112
Liberating Through Forgiveness: A Path to Inner Harmony... 115
Harmonizing Your Space: A Cleansing Ritual............. 116
Unlocking Your Potential: The Power of Empowerments and Clearing 118

Navigating Life's Path: Setting Clear Intentions
and Goals 120

Charting Your Course: Goal-Setting and
Manifestation 123

Guiding Principles for Goal Setting: Nurturing Your
Inner Garden 125

Harnessing the Power of Pioneering Thinking:
Weaving Your Dreams 128

Charting Your Destiny: The Art of Treasure Mapping 130

Crafting Your Vision: A Gallery of Treasure Map Ideas . 132

Harmony of Health and Beauty: A Journey
Through Pioneering Thinking 135

The Art of Inner Beauty and Wellness: An Indian
Perspective 137

Group Pioneering Thinking: A Collective Journey
Towards Manifestation 139

Harmonious Relationships Through Pioneering
Thinking: Nurturing the Bonds of Unity 142

Part 5
Divine Expression: Unleashing Creativity for Manifestation 146

The Essence of Creative Consciousness:
Unleashing Divine Potential 148

Unveiling Your Divine Purpose: Illuminating the Path 150

Crafting the Masterpiece of Your Life: An Artistic
Odyssey 152

Gratitude: Nurturing the Garden of Inspiration 154

Part 6
Integration of Technology for Manifesting Dreams ... 157

Virtual Reality (VR) Visualization 159

Mind-Machine Interface (MMI) Meditation 161

Artificial Intelligence (AI) Personalization 163
Living Mindfully: Embodying the Synthesis 166
Embracing Holistic Integration: The Synergy of
Tradition and Innovation 168
Harmonizing Tradition and Innovation: A Roadmap
for Manifestation Mastery 170
Embracing the Journey: Manifestation as a Way
of Life 171
Wishing You Good Luck and Persistence.................... 173

Recommended resources **176**

Part 1

The Dreams: Unveiling the Power of Willpower

Dear Comrades in the Quest for Fulfillment

I am inspired to share with you through this book the profound journey of self-discovery and transformation that I have experienced. My path has been illuminated by the rich interplay of Eastern philosophical wisdom and Western psychological insights, leading me to the treasure trove of Pioneering Thinking.

I stand before you not as a master but as a fellow student in the art of willpower. This journey has unveiled to me the limitless potential of the human imagination, a force as boundless as the universe itself. My exploration into this realm is an ongoing adventure, revealing the infinite possibilities that lie within our grasp.

This book serves as a foundational guide and a practical workbook for those eager to embark on the path of Pioneering Thinking. The insights here are not purely of my creation but a synthesis of the most effective ideas and practices I have encountered in my journey of learning.

The roots of this wisdom can be traced back to the ancient Indian philosophy of 'Sankalpa' - the power of intention and willpower. This philosophy aligns with the essence of this book, which aims to harness the power of our imagination to shape our reality.

Pioneering Thinking utilizes our innate ability to create mental images and feelings, channeling them towards manifesting our desires. This practice transcends mere daydreaming; it is an active engagement with the universe to bring forth the life we envision.

For instance, if you find yourself in an unsatisfactory job, willpower can be a powerful tool. Picture yourself in your ideal work environment, feel the satisfaction of doing fulfilling work, and experience the harmony in professional relationships, as if it's already your reality.

This book is not about manipulating external circumstances or controlling others but about dissolving internal barriers to achieve harmony and fulfillment. It requires an open mind and the willingness to entertain new possibilities.

Pioneering Thinking is a form of magic in its truest sense. It aligns with the natural laws of the universe, allowing us to tap into its creative power. Like witnessing a breathtaking sunset for the first time, the initial awe gives way to understanding and appreciation of the natural processes at work.

As you delve into the practices outlined in this book, you may find that what once seemed miraculous becomes a natural, integrated part of your life. It's a journey of turning dreams into reality, a journey where the wonders you manifest may exceed your wildest dreams.

With an open heart and mind, I invite you to embark on this transformative journey. May the art of Pioneering Thinking enrich your life, just as it has mine, opening doors to new realms of possibilities.

Unveiling the Power of Imagination: The Essence of Pioneering Thinking

In the realm of ancient Indian philosophy, there is a deep understanding that the universe around us is a manifestation of energy, a concept echoed in the teachings of the Vedas and Upanishads. This fundamental belief forms the cornerstone of my exploration into the world of Pioneering Thinking.

At its heart, Pioneering Thinking is the art of harnessing the power of our imagination to sculpt our reality. It isn't a novel or esoteric idea but a natural ability we wield, often unconsciously. It's about channeling the boundless energy of thought, which is lighter and more malleable than the denser energies of the physical world.

Throughout my journey, I've realized that our thoughts, being vibrational energy, have a magnetic quality. They attract energies of similar frequencies. This phenomenon is apparent in the serendipities of life, like unexpectedly encountering someone you've just thought of, or stumbling upon information that perfectly aligns with your needs.

The principle that 'form follows idea' is pivotal in understanding Pioneering Thinking. Every creation begins as a thought. An artist envisions a painting before the brush hits the canvas, a chef imagines a dish before it's cooked, and an architect designs a building before it's constructed. These thoughts act as blueprints, drawing in the energy to materialize them into physical reality.

Furthermore, the Law of Radiation and Attraction teaches us that the universe mirrors our thoughts and emotions. Our deepest convictions, fears, and aspirations shape the reality that unfolds around us. Hence, harboring positive, constructive thoughts can lead to favorable outcomes in our lives.

Pioneering Thinking, therefore, is not merely wishful thinking. It is an active process of transforming our deepest attitudes and beliefs, thereby reshaping our life experiences. In practicing Pioneering Thinking, we often uncover and dissolve limiting beliefs, paving the way for a life filled with greater joy, fulfillment, and love.

Initially, Pioneering Thinking might be a practice reserved for specific times and goals. However, as one delves deeper, it becomes an integral part of our thought process, a continuous state of consciousness where we recognize our role as creators of our reality.

The ultimate aim of Pioneering Thinking is to transform every moment into an opportunity for creation, choosing the most fulfilling and enriching paths. It is a journey of not just envisioning a better life but actively creating it, one thought at a time.

Manifesting Dreams: The Art of Willpower

In the heart of India's ancient wisdom lies the practice of 'Dhyana' or meditation, a technique akin to what we know today as Pioneering Thinking. This simple yet profound exercise is rooted in the belief that our imagination is a powerful tool for manifesting our deepest desires.

Let's embark on a journey of Pioneering Thinking. Choose a desire that resonates with you, something tangible and within the realm of possibility. It could be an object you wish to possess, an event you aspire to experience, a situation you want to be in, or an aspect of your life you wish to enhance.

Find a peaceful spot where you won't be disturbed. Settle into a comfortable position, sitting or lying down. Begin by relaxing your body completely. Imagine a wave of relaxation starting from your toes, slowly rising to the top of your head. With each breath, draw in calmness and exhale tension. Count down gently from ten to one, sinking into deeper relaxation at each number.

Now, with your body and mind in a state of relaxation, vividly picture your desire. If it's an object, see yourself holding it, using it, cherishing it. If it's a situation, place yourself within it, feeling the emotions, hearing the sounds, and seeing the environment around you.

Spend as much time as you need in this willpower. It should be a delightful and uplifting experience, like a child lost in the anticipation of their birthday.

While maintaining this image, affirm your vision with positive statements. Say to yourself: "Here I am, enjoying a rejuvenating weekend in the hills. What a refreshing getaway!" or "The view from my new, airy apartment is breathtaking." or "Day by day, I am learning to embrace and love myself as I am."

These empowerments, or 'Sankalpas' as known in Sanskrit, reinforce your willpower.

To conclude, you might add: "This, or something even better, now unfolds in my life, perfectly aligned for the highest good of all."

If doubts arise, let them pass like clouds in the sky, acknowledging them but returning to your positive willpowers and empowerments.

Engage in this practice daily, for as long as it brings you joy and peace, be it five minutes or thirty. Over time, you may find that what you visualize begins to manifest in your life, a testament to the power of Pioneering Thinking.

This exercise, simple in its essence, can become profoundly effective with practice and understanding. It's a journey into the depths of your mind and the vast potential of your imagination.

The Essence of Tranquility in Willpower

In the ancient Indian tradition, relaxation and meditation hold a paramount place, reminiscent of the practices outlined in the Upanishads for achieving a deeper connection with the self. Embracing this wisdom is crucial when embarking on the journey of Pioneering Thinking. The state of profound relaxation is not just beneficial for the mind and body, but it significantly enhances the effectiveness of willpower techniques.

When we relax deeply, our brain's activity shifts from the bustling 'beta' level to the serene 'alpha' level. This shift is more than just a change in brain waves; it's a doorway to a healthier state of being, where the mind's power to influence our reality is greatly amplified. In this state, the hustle of thoughts gives way to a more potent form of consciousness, capable of molding our environment with greater efficacy than our active waking state.

If you already have a preferred method of attaining this deep state of relaxation, such as meditation or a specific breathing technique, continue to embrace it. For those seeking guidance, the age-old practice of deep, rhythmic breathing, relaxing each muscle group sequentially, and a gentle countdown from ten to one can be profoundly effective. For individuals finding physical relaxation challenging, exploring yoga or meditation can provide invaluable skills not only for Pioneering Thinking but also for overall well-being.

The ideal times for practicing Pioneering Thinking are during the twilight zones of our consciousness - just before drifting to sleep and upon awakening. During these moments, the mind and body naturally inhabit the relaxed, receptive alpha state. If you prefer to practice in bed, ensure you maintain an alert posture to avoid dozing off. Sitting with a straight spine can aid in energy flow and deepen your relaxation.

Incorporating a brief session of meditation and willpower around midday can also be incredibly beneficial. It acts as a reset button, infusing the remainder of your day with tranquility and focus.

Remember, the journey of Pioneering Thinking is not just about the destination but also about nurturing a harmonious balance within the mind, body, and spirit. This balance is the key to unlocking our full potential in shaping our lives and our world.

Exploring the Landscape of Willpower: A Journey Within

In the profound depths of Indian philosophy, there's an understanding that our inner world shapes our outer reality, a concept that resonates with the practice of Pioneering Thinking. This process involves using the power of your mind to manifest your deepest desires and aspirations.

Pioneering Thinking isn't just about 'seeing' with the mind's eye. It's about experiencing a thought or a desire in whichever way feels most natural to you. When you close your eyes to visualize, you might not see vivid pictures, and that's perfectly fine. Some people visualize through sensations, emotions, or a simple sense of knowing. This diversity in experiencing willpower is a reflection of our unique ways of connecting with the world - some of us are more visual, others more attuned to sounds or feelings.

If you're unsure of how to begin, try this simple exercise:

1. Find a quiet, comfortable space and close your eyes. Take a few deep breaths and let your body relax from head to toe.
2. Think of a familiar space, like your bedroom or a cozy corner of your home. Recall the colors, textures, and how the light falls in that space. Imagine yourself walking into this room and settling down in your favorite spot.
3. Now, bring to mind a recent enjoyable experience. Relive the physical sensations, the tastes, the sounds, or the emotions of that moment.
4. Picture yourself in a serene natural setting - perhaps a meadow with soft grass under a clear blue sky or a peaceful forest with the gentle rustle of leaves. Create this place in your mind, filling in as many details as you can.

The method you naturally gravitate towards in this exercise is your personal way of visualizing.

In Pioneering Thinking, we engage in two modes: the receptive and the active. In the receptive mode, we allow images and impressions to flow to us without consciously constructing them. In the active mode, we deliberately create and shape these images. Both are essential and enhance our ability to visualize effectively.

Occasionally, individuals may find it challenging to visualize, often stemming from internal fears or past experiences. For instance, a man might struggle with willpower due to a past emotional experience he's not ready to face, or a woman might find it hard to visualize until she addresses and releases deep-seated childhood emotions.

If difficulties arise during willpower, the key is to confront them head-on. Facing our fears, rather than avoiding them, diminishes their power over us. In cases where the emotions or memories are overwhelming, seeking support from a counselor or therapist can be immensely beneficial.

Remember, Pioneering Thinking is a skill that improves with practice. It's a journey of discovering your inner world and harnessing its power to shape your life. If willpower proves challenging, empowerments can be a powerful alternative, as they too harness the power of thought to manifest desires.

In this journey of willpower, you are not just imagining; you are creating. Each thought, each image, each feeling is a step towards manifesting your desires into reality.

The Art of Manifesting Dreams: A Step-by-Step Guide

In the vibrant tradition of Indian philosophy, where the power of the mind is celebrated, the practice of Pioneering Thinking is a technique akin to 'Sankalpa' in Yoga - setting an intention or resolution. Here are four fundamental steps to effectively harness this ancient wisdom for modern aspirations.

1. **Define Your Aspiration**: Begin by identifying a goal that resonates with you. It could be as tangible as acquiring a new skill, as personal as improving your well-being, or as ambitious as contributing to community welfare. Initially, select objectives that seem achievable in the near future to avoid internal resistance and to cultivate a sense of accomplishment. As your proficiency in willpower grows, you can gradually tackle more complex or long-term goals.

2. **Craft a Vivid Mental Image**: Develop a detailed mental picture of your goal as if it's already achieved. Imagine yourself living that reality – the sights, sounds, emotions, and textures. Integrate as many specifics as you can to make the willpower as real as possible. Optionally, create a physical representation of your goal, like a vision board, to

reinforce and clarify your mental image. This step mirrors the Indian practice of 'Dharana' - concentration, where focused attention brings clarity and power to your intentions.

3. **Regularly Focus on Your Goal**: Integrate your vision into your daily life. Regularly revisit your mental image, not only during quiet meditation but also casually throughout your day. This repeated focus helps to embed your aspiration into your subconscious, gradually making it a part of your lived experience. However, maintain a relaxed and effortless approach to avoid creating mental strain or resistance.

4. **Energize with Positive Empowerments**: Infuse your goal with positivity. Use empowerments - positive, assertive statements - to reinforce the belief in the realization of your goal. Visualize yourself achieving it and feel the emotions associated with its fulfillment. For the moments of practice, suspend any skepticism or doubts, and immerse yourself in the certainty of your success. This process is akin to 'Pratipaksha Bhavana' in Yogic philosophy, where one cultivates the opposite thought or attitude to counteract negativity.

Remember, it's natural for goals to evolve or change; it's part of our growth. If you find your interest waning, acknowledge it, and feel free to redirect your focus. This awareness prevents feelings of failure and keeps your practice aligned with your true aspirations.

Finally, when you achieve your goal, consciously acknowledge and celebrate your success. Recognize the fruition of your efforts and express gratitude to the universe for facilitating your journey. This step is crucial for it completes the cycle of manifestation, allowing you to move forward with confidence and clarity.

Through these steps, you can tap into the timeless wisdom of Pioneering Thinking, blending ancient Indian spiritual practices with contemporary techniques to manifest your deepest desires.

Harnessing Willpower for Universal Good

In the rich tapestry of Indian spiritual tradition, there's a deep understanding that our thoughts and actions are intricately connected to the universe's flow, a concept echoing the ancient law of Karma. When we delve into the practice of Pioneering Thinking, it's crucial to recognize that this powerful tool is most effective when aligned with the greater good and our highest aspirations.

Pioneering Thinking acts as a key to unlock or dissolve the self-imposed barriers to the universe's natural state of harmony, abundance, and love. It reaches its true potential only when used for positive and benevolent purposes, benefiting not just the individual but all beings.

The misuse of this potent technique for selfish or harmful ends is fundamentally a misapprehension of the karmic law, often summarized as "As you sow, so shall you reap." Any intention set into the universe, whether it's for healing, love, or otherwise, circles back to the originator. This principle underscores that when we use Pioneering Thinking to foster love and serve the highest good of others and ourselves, we naturally attract more love, joy, and success into our lives.

To ensure that your willpower practices are aligned with this principle, it's advisable to incorporate a phrase like, "This, or something better, now manifests for me in totally satisfying and harmonious ways, for the highest good of all concerned." This affirmation ensures that your desires are not only in harmony with your well-being but also with the collective good.

Consider, for example, visualizing a job promotion. Rather than picturing someone losing their job to make way for your opportunity, envision a scenario where everyone's path progresses positively. Visualize the person ahead of you moving on to something that brings them greater fulfillment, thereby creating a harmonious transition for all involved. In doing so, you're entrusting the finer details to the universe's wisdom, confident that the outcome will be beneficial for all.

Through this practice, Pioneering Thinking transcends personal gain and becomes a tool for contributing positively to the world, weaving individual aspirations with the universal fabric of harmony and well-being.

Manifesting Dreams: A Guide to Positive Empowerments

In the heart of India's ancient wisdom, the power of words and thoughts in shaping our reality is profoundly recognized, aligning closely with the teachings of the Upanishads. This essence is embodied in the practice of Pioneering Thinking and the use of empowerments - a powerful combination for personal transformation.

Empowerments are potent, positive declarations that reinforce the manifestation of our desires. They are not mere words, but tools to solidify what we envision in our minds. Like a sculptor chiseling away at stone, empowerments help carve our thoughts into reality.

Our minds are like fertile gardens where seeds of thoughts sprout into reality. Often, this internal dialogue unconsciously shapes our life experiences. Through meditation, we can observe this ceaseless stream of thoughts, identifying patterns that may have rooted in our psyche since childhood, influencing our present.

Empowerments serve as a transformative practice, replacing outdated or negative thought patterns with uplifting and life-affirming beliefs. Even a few minutes of daily empowerments can counterbalance years of ingrained mental habits. Whenever you catch yourself in a spiral of negative thinking, counter it with an affirmation.

For instance, if you find yourself thinking, "I'm not capable of achieving this," immediately replace it with, "I possess the strength and ability to accomplish my goals."

Here are some empowerments that can be tailored to various aspects of life:

1. Personal Growth:
   - "Every day, in every way, I am becoming better and better."
   - "I am whole, perfect, strong, powerful, loving, harmonious, and happy."

2. Love and Relationships:
   - "I attract loving and caring people into my life."
   - "My relationships are filled with love and respect."

3. Health and Well-being:
   - "I am vibrant, healthy, and full of energy."
   - "Every cell in my body vibrates with health and energy."

4. Abundance and Prosperity:
   - "Abundance flows into my life effortlessly."

- "I am a magnet for success and good fortune."
5. Work and Career:
    - "I am passionate about my work and valued for my contributions."
    - "Opportunities for growth and success are available to me at all times."

Remember, empowerments are most effective when they resonate with your inner truth and are expressed in the present tense, as though they are already a reality. Repeat them with conviction, and envision the affirmation as already manifested.

In the journey of using empowerments, it's essential to maintain patience and trust in the process. Like nurturing a plant, empowerments require time to take root and flourish.

Empowerments are not just a tool for personal gain; they align our individual aspirations with the universal flow, creating harmony and balance in our lives and the world around us.

The Art of Crafting Empowerments: Guidelines for Positive Manifestation

In the rich tapestry of Indian spiritual philosophy, empowerments are akin to 'Sankalpa,' a Sanskrit word that means an intention formed by the heart and mind. Here are some vital pointers to remember when practicing the art of empowerments, weaving them into the fabric of your daily life for transformative change.

1. **Embrace the Present**: Frame your empowerments in the present tense, as if the desired state is already a reality. Instead of saying, "I will achieve success," affirm, "I am successful in my endeavors." This approach is rooted in the belief that creation starts within before manifesting

externally, a concept echoed in the Upanishads where the inner world is seen as a precursor to the external reality.

2. **Focus on Positivity**: Phrase your empowerments positively, focusing on what you wish to attract rather than what you want to avoid. For instance, instead of saying, "I am not stressed," use, "I am calm and at peace." This ensures that your mind visualizes positive outcomes.

3. **Simplicity and Emotion**: Keep your empowerments concise and emotionally charged. A simple, heartfelt affirmation has more power than a lengthy, complex one. The emotional energy behind the words is what embeds them deeply into your subconscious.

4. **Personal Relevance**: Choose empowerments that resonate personally with you. What works for one may not work for another. An affirmation should feel uplifting and empowering. If it doesn't, modify it until it feels right, keeping in mind your unique journey and aspirations.

5. **New Beginnings**: View each affirmation as creating something new rather than modifying what exists. This perspective helps avoid resistance and struggle, aligning with the principle of 'Pravritti,' where every moment is an opportunity for creation and growth.

6. **Harmony with Emotions**: Empowerments are not meant to suppress or contradict your emotions. Acknowledge and accept your feelings, even the negative ones. Empowerments serve to gradually shift your perspective, leading to more fulfilling experiences.

7. **Believe in Possibilities**: While affirming, try to foster a sense of belief, even if temporarily. Suspend doubts and immerse yourself fully in the possibility that your empowerments can manifest. This belief is the seed from

which the reality of your empowerments can sprout and grow.

Remember, the practice of empowerments is an exercise in shaping your inner world to reflect in your outer reality. It's about aligning your thoughts with the universal energy, as taught in ancient Indian wisdom, to bring about positive change in your life.

Manifesting Intentions: Overcoming Doubts with Empowerments

In the rich tapestry of Indian spirituality, much like the teachings of the Upanishads, the power of empowerments is akin to invoking the divine within us to shape our destiny. Here's how to effectively use empowerments, especially when faced with doubts or negative thoughts, drawing inspiration from the profound wisdom of ancient Indian practices.

1. **Clearing Negative Thoughts**: If doubts or resistance hinder your affirmation practice, consider engaging in clearing techniques outlined in later sections of this book. These methods help in releasing the mental blocks, paving the way for more effective empowerments.

2. **Feel the Power of Creation**: Rather than mechanically repeating empowerments, imbue them with the belief that you possess the power to manifest your desires. This conviction is central to the effectiveness of your empowerments, as it aligns with the Indian philosophy of 'Atma Shakti' – the belief in the inner power and strength of the soul.

3. **Combine with Willpower**: Empowerments work wonderfully when used alongside willpower techniques. During your willpower sessions, include empowerments to

reinforce the imagery, creating a powerful synergy for manifesting your goals.

4. **Incorporate Spiritual References**: For many, empowerments resonate deeper when connected to a higher spiritual source. Phrases invoking divine energy, such as 'God,' 'Goddess,' 'Universe,' 'Higher Power,' or 'Divine Love,' add a profound dimension to your empowerments. This practice draws from the Indian tradition of recognizing and honoring the divine force that permeates all of existence.

Here are a few examples of spiritually infused empowerments:

- "Within me lies the boundless creative energy of the Goddess, shaping my world."
- "The divine love in me is manifesting my desires here and now."
- "Through me, the Ganesha consciousness is creating miracles in my life."
- "I am united with the Great Spirit, guiding me in all my actions."
- "My higher self leads me in all I do, bringing forth the best outcomes."
- "God's presence within me transforms my world, manifesting beauty and goodness."
- "Every day, I am grateful to Mother Earth for her nurturing and sustenance."
- "Surrounded by the light of the Divine, I am a channel for love, power, and grace."

Remember, the key to effective empowerments lies in the belief and emotion infused in them. When you align your empowerments with the universal energies, as taught in the ancient wisdom of India, you harness the power to transform your thoughts into reality.

Embracing the Spiritual Paradox: Balancing Desire and Detachment

In the profound wisdom of Indian spirituality, there exists a seeming paradox between the pursuit of personal desires and the concept of detachment, a theme recurrent in the Upanishads and the Bhagavad Gita. This paradox often puzzles those on a spiritual journey, especially when they encounter the practice of Pioneering Thinking.

This paradox stems from the apparent contradiction between living in the 'here and now,' letting go of attachments and desires, and the concept of actively creating and aspiring for personal goals. However, this apparent contradiction dissolves when viewed from a deeper, spiritual perspective.

In our culture, many have lost touch with their spiritual essence, leading to an inner sense of powerlessness. This feeling drives a relentless pursuit of control or influence over external circumstances, as a means to fill an inner void. We become goal-oriented, emotionally attached to external entities, perpetually striving to manipulate our environment to achieve happiness.

This state of constant striving often leads to frustration, as goals achieved do not always bring the inner fulfillment anticipated. It is at this point that many embark on a spiritual quest, seeking something more profound and fulfilling.

In this journey, the first lesson is often about letting go. We learn to relax our relentless pursuit, to stop manipulating, and to experience being. This process of 'letting go' is akin to the Buddhist concept of detachment and aligns with the Christian notion of surrendering to God's will. It's a liberating experience, allowing us to just 'be' and to let the world around us also 'be.'

The reconciliation of this paradox lies in understanding that as we connect with our inner spiritual essence, we fill the void from within. This connection brings about a sense of wholeness and empowerment, eliminating the desperate need to control external circumstances for fulfillment.

Once this inner fulfillment is attained, the pursuit of personal goals no longer comes from a place of emptiness or desperation. Instead, it becomes an expression of our joy, creativity, and spiritual essence. We set goals not because we are incomplete without them, but because they represent the natural extension of our inner abundance and creativity.

Pioneering Thinking thus becomes a tool not for grasping at desires, but for expressing our innate creative powers in harmony with the universe. It aligns our personal aspirations with the flow of universal energy, striking a balance between desire and detachment, between personal will and the greater cosmic order.

In the heart of this spiritual paradox lies the key to a fulfilling journey – where we are neither blindly attached to our desires nor completely detached from the world, but in a state of dynamic balance, embracing the beauty of both being and becoming.

Navigating Life's River: The Journey of Self-Empowerment and Willpower

In the profound wisdom of Indian spirituality, often echoed in the sacred texts like the Upanishads, there's an understanding that we are the creators of our own life experiences. As you delve deeper into this realization, you begin to channel your innate creative energy more purposefully, leading to a life rich with rewarding experiences for yourself and others. This understanding is akin to recognizing that life, in its essence, is abundant, joyful, and fulfilling, and that attaining what we truly desire is a natural part of our existence.

To illustrate this further, consider life as a vast, flowing river. Initially, many of us cling to the banks, fearful of the river's current. However, a pivotal moment comes when we decide to let go and trust the river's flow. This act of surrender, of "going with the flow," is exhilarating and liberating.

Once acclimatized to the river's flow, we can start to navigate consciously. We can choose our path, steer around obstacles, and decide which tributaries of life to explore, all while harmoniously flowing with life's current. This metaphor encapsulates the balance of accepting life as it is (being in the now) and consciously directing our journey towards our chosen goals.

Pioneering Thinking becomes a powerful tool at this stage. It allows us to craft our journey, not as a struggle against life's current, but as a conscious co-creation with the universe. It's about aligning our personal desires with the universal flow, recognizing that we are not just passive onlookers but active participants in the tapestry of life.

Moreover, Pioneering Thinking isn't limited to material aspirations. It's a versatile tool that can be employed for spiritual growth. Visualize yourself as a more open, relaxed individual, living in the moment and continually connected to your inner essence. This practice can transform your perception of life, opening you to experiences filled with awareness, joy, and fulfillment.

As you embark on this journey, may you be blessed with all that your heart desires, finding harmony between being and becoming, between the material and the spiritual, in the ever-flowing river of life.

Part 2

Unlocking the Power Within: The Art of Pioneering Thinking

In the sacred verses of the Bhagavad Gita, Lord Krishna imparts timeless wisdom to Arjuna: "Whatever you ask for with a pure heart, I provide. Whatever you seek with devotion, you shall find. Whatever doors you knock upon, I shall open." This profound teaching resonates with the universal principle echoed in the Bhagavad Gita and the Upanishads, emphasizing the potency of focused intention and unwavering faith.

The Ancient Guidance: Seeking Answers Within

In the heart of India's spiritual heritage lies the Bhagavad Gita, where Lord Krishna's words serve as a beacon of guidance. His counsel to "ask, seek, and knock" reflects the ancient practice of harnessing the power of Pioneering Thinking to manifest one's deepest desires.

The Yogic Path: Willpower in the Upanishads

The Upanishads, revered as the ultimate source of spiritual knowledge, further illuminate the path of Pioneering Thinking. "Tat Tvam Asi," they proclaim, meaning "You are that." This profound revelation underscores the connection between the seeker and the divine, highlighting the innate ability to manifest desires through focused intention.

Modern Insights: Aligning with the Law of Attraction

In the modern world, the Law of Attraction echoes the age-old wisdom found in India's scriptures. This universal law posits that like attracts like, emphasizing the importance of maintaining a positive mindset and visualizing one's goals with unwavering belief.

Stories of Manifestation: From Ancient Tales to Modern Realities

Throughout India's rich tapestry of legends and epics, stories abound of individuals who, through the power of Pioneering Thinking and devout seeking, manifested their desires. From the tale of Lord Rama's unwavering determination to rescue Sita to the modern narratives of individuals achieving their dreams, these stories serve as living testaments to the transformative potential of willpower.

Harnessing Modern Tools: Technology and Willpower

In today's digital age, cutting-edge technology and scientific research support the practice of Pioneering Thinking. Studies on neuroplasticity reveal the brain's ability to rewire itself based on focused mental imagery, aligning with the Vedic concept of "Sankalpa," the power of intention.

The Practice Unveiled: Pioneering Thinking as a Spiritual Tool

As we venture forth on the path of Pioneering Thinking, we pay homage to the profound wisdom of the Bhagavad Gita, the Upanishads, and the principle of Karma. By harmonizing our sankalpas (intentions) with the eternal truths, we unlock the boundless potential dwelling within us, echoing the ancient teachings of the Vedas. Just as it is said in the scriptures, 'Aham Brahmasmi' (I am the universe), we realize that by seeking within, we shall receive; by exploring the depths of our consciousness, we shall discover; and by persistently striving, the doors of divine grace shall open unto us. Through the practice of Pioneering Thinking, we connect with the divine reservoir of our inner strength, where the manifestation of our desires unfolds as a sublime union between the seeker and the cosmic consciousness.

Embracing Universal Abundance: The Law of Seeking and Receiving

In the eternal wisdom of Indian philosophy, as articulated in the timeless scriptures such as the Upanishads, there exists a profound recognition of the interconnectedness between our intentions and the universe's response. This ancient understanding mirrors the essence of the universal principles expounded in the Upanishads and Vedas.

"Invoke the divine, and grace shall shower upon you; pursue the path of truth, and you shall uncover its secrets; request guidance, and the way forward shall be illuminated. For every seeker who invokes the divine, blessings flow abundantly; for every truth-seeker, the mysteries of existence unfold; and for every sincere seeker of knowledge, the path to enlightenment unveils itself.

This profound teaching is not just a spiritual concept but a universal principle. It suggests that the act of asking sets into motion the universe's mechanisms to fulfill those desires. It's about aligning our intentions with the cosmic flow, understanding that the universe is not just a passive backdrop but an active, responsive entity.

In your journey of seeking, remember that the universe responds not only to our spoken requests but also to the intentions and desires held in our hearts. Every sincere aspiration is like a seed planted in the cosmic soil, which, given the right conditions, will sprout and flourish.

This principle is mirrored in the practice of 'Sankalpa' in Yoga, where setting a heartfelt intention is considered the first step towards realization. It's about harmonizing our individual will with the universal will, understanding that our personal desires, when in tune with the greater good, are supported by the cosmic energies.

So, as you embark on your path, whether it be in pursuit of knowledge, personal growth, spiritual enlightenment, or material success, hold onto this ancient wisdom. Ask with clarity and conviction, seek with an open heart, and knock with persistence and faith. The universe, in its abundant generosity, responds to the earnest seeker, opening doors and revealing paths that lead not just to the fulfillment of desires but also to a deeper understanding of the cosmic dance of creation and fulfillment.

May your journey of seeking and receiving be blessed with wisdom, abundance, and fulfillment, as you walk the path illuminated by this timeless truth.

Integrating Pioneering Thinking into Everyday Life

Drawing inspiration from the ancient wisdom of Indian philosophy, similar to the principles elucidated in the Upanishads, Pioneering Thinking is a powerful tool that can bring about significant positive changes in your life. The key to harnessing its full potential is to make it a consistent and integral part of your daily routine.

1. **Regular Practice**: The essence of Pioneering Thinking is rooted in its regular practice. It's most beneficial to incorporate a session of Pioneering Thinking into your daily routine, ideally in the tranquil moments of the morning and the reflective quiet of the evening. These are the times when your mind is most receptive to the power of

willpower. If possible, a midday session can also be highly effective in maintaining a positive mindset throughout the day.

2. **Deep Relaxation as a Foundation**: Begin each willpower session with a period of deep relaxation. This could involve techniques such as deep breathing, progressive muscle relaxation, or meditation. This initial relaxation sets the stage for a more profound and effective willpower experience.

3. **Application in Various Situations**: Pioneering Thinking is versatile and can be applied to a myriad of situations, whether it's solving problems, overcoming worries, or enhancing your personal and professional life. Whenever you encounter a challenge, pause and consider how Pioneering Thinking can offer a solution or a new perspective.

4. **Create a Willpower Habit**: Encourage yourself to use Pioneering Thinking spontaneously throughout your day. Every situation, be it a challenge or an opportunity, can benefit from the clarity and positivity that willpower brings.

5. **Patience and Persistence**: It's important to remember that changing deep-rooted thought patterns takes time. Most of us have spent years cultivating these patterns, and transforming them into positive ones is a gradual process. If you don't see immediate results, don't be disheartened. Patience and persistence are key.

6. **Overcoming Underlying Negative Beliefs**: Be aware of any underlying negative beliefs or attitudes that might be impeding your progress with Pioneering Thinking. Tackling these underlying issues can significantly enhance the effectiveness of your willpower practice.

Pioneering Thinking is much like planting a seed in the fertile ground of your consciousness. With regular care, patience, and the right conditions, this seed will grow and flourish, transforming your life in alignment with your deepest desires and aspirations. As you practice, remember that you are tapping into a universal power, one that connects your personal vision to the cosmic dance of creation and manifestation.

Incorporating Pioneering Thinking into Your Life

In the diverse and rich philosophical landscape of India, akin to the teachings of the Upanishads, the practice of Pioneering Thinking emerges as a powerful tool for personal transformation. Here are some insights into making this practice a natural part of your life, blending ancient wisdom with modern understanding.

1. **The Power of Brief Sessions**: Pioneering Thinking is a potent process. Even a brief session of focused, positive meditation can counteract long-standing negative patterns. Just like the ancient practice of 'Dhyana' (meditation) in Indian philosophy, a few minutes of dedicated willpower can bring profound shifts in your consciousness.

2. **Patience and Continuity**: Remember, the reality you live in now is the culmination of a lifetime's experiences and thoughts. Instantaneous change is rare. Like the slow unfolding of a lotus, changes will manifest gradually yet surely. With continued practice and understanding, what may initially seem miraculous will become a natural part of your life's journey.

3. **Inspirational Reading**: Regularly immerse yourself in literature that uplifts and supports your highest aspirations. This practice can be a beacon during challenging times,

much like the wisdom imparted in ancient Indian scriptures that guide and illuminate.

4. **Community and Support**: Engaging with a community or friends who share your journey towards conscious living can be incredibly supportive. Participating in workshops, support groups, or therapy sessions not only provides you with encouragement but also allows you to offer support to others.

5. **Variety in Techniques**: The chapters ahead offer a range of techniques, exercises, and meditations. Choose what resonates with you. The practice of Pioneering Thinking is multi-faceted, and different approaches may suit different individuals or situations. Trust your intuition and be drawn to the practices that feel right for you.

6. **Intuitive Guidance**: If a particular technique, like empowerments, feels forced or ineffective, it might be beneficial to try a clearing process, seek inner guidance, or simply take a break and focus elsewhere. What is effective in one scenario may not be in another, and what works for one person may differ for another.

7. **Ease Over Effort**: Trust your feelings. If a practice feels like a strain or effort, it might not be the right approach at that time. If it feels enlightening, empowering, and invigorating, it's likely to be beneficial.

In conclusion, Pioneering Thinking is not just a technique but a way of life. It's about blending your personal energy with the cosmic rhythm, creating a life that resonates with your deepest aspirations. As you embark on this journey, let the ancient wisdom of India guide you, reminding you that you are an integral part of the universal tapestry, capable of weaving your own destiny.

The Essence of Essence, Action, and Possession in Life's Journey

In the diverse and rich philosophical landscape of India, akin to the profound insights of the Upanishads, life can be understood through the interplay of three fundamental aspects: essence, action, and possession.

1. **Essence:** The Core of Existence: At the heart of our existence is 'essence' – a state of conscious presence and awareness. It's akin to the state of 'Satchitananda' in Hindu philosophy, which represents the pure essence of being – truth, consciousness, and bliss. This state is experienced in moments of complete immersion in the present, where one feels a sense of completeness and inner peace.

2. **Action:** The Expression of Vitality: 'Action' is the dynamic aspect of life, characterized by movement and engagement. It springs from the creative energy that animates all living beings. This is reflective of the concept of 'Prana' in Indian philosophy, the vital life force that propels us into action and fuels our vitality.

3. **Possession:** The Art of Relationship: 'Possession' pertains to our relationships with people and things in the world. It encompasses our ability to accept, allow, and coexist with various elements of our external environment. This aspect resonates with the idea of 'Lila', the divine play of the universe, where we interact with the myriad forms and experiences life offers.

Together, these three aspects form a harmonious triangle, each supporting and balancing the others. They are not contradictory but coexist and complement each other in our journey of life.

Often, people mistakenly pursue life in reverse – seeking to possess more in the belief that it will enable them to act as they desire, and consequently be happier. However, the true path begins with 'essence' – realizing and embracing your true self. From this state of authenticity, your 'action' becomes a natural expression of your essence. This, in turn, leads to 'possessing' what you truly desire, not just materially but in richness of experience and relationships.

Pioneering Thinking serves as a bridge connecting these aspects. It helps us to embrace our true 'essence', focus our actions ('action'), and align our experiences and possessions ('possession') with our deepest values and aspirations.

The journey of life encompasses the balance of essence, action, and possession. By starting with self-realization, moving through purposeful action, and culminating in harmonious existence, we align ourselves with the universal flow, creating a life of fulfillment and harmony.

Harmonizing Desire, Belief, and Acceptance: Key Pillars of Pioneering Thinking

In the context of Indian philosophical wisdom, akin to the profound teachings of the Upanishads, the success of Pioneering Thinking in one's life can be seen as a confluence of three crucial internal elements: desire, belief, and acceptance. These elements resonate with the core principles of Sankalpa (intention or resolve), Shraddha (faith), and Samarpan (surrender) in Indian spiritual practices.

1. **Desire – The Seed of Aspiration**: At the foundation is a genuine desire for the goal you wish to achieve through willpower. This is similar to the concept of 'Sankalpa' in yoga and meditation, where setting a heartfelt intention is seen as the first step towards manifestation. Reflect deeply

and ask, "Is this what I truly yearn for at the deepest level of my heart?"

2. **Belief – The Power of Conviction**: The strength of your belief in both the goal and your ability to attain it is crucial. This aligns with 'Shraddha', a Sanskrit term implying faith or trust. It's about having conviction in the possibilities that life offers. Question yourself, "Do I firmly believe that this goal is attainable, and do I trust in my capability to realize it?"

3. **Acceptance – The Art of Allowing**: Finally, there must be an openness to receive and welcome what you are aiming for. In Indian spirituality, this is akin to 'Samarpan', or surrender, where you open yourself to receive the grace of the universe. Reflect on whether you are truly ready to embrace the realization of your goals: "Am I fully prepared to accept and welcome this into my life?"

The synthesis of these three elements forms what is known as your 'intention'. When your intention is clear, robust, and unambiguous, embodying a deep desire, unwavering belief, and complete willingness to accept, the manifestation of your goals becomes more probable and potent.

In any situation, evaluate the strength of your intention. If you find it wavering or unclear, delve deeper to unearth any underlying doubts, fears, or internal conflicts. Sometimes, hesitation can be a signal to acknowledge and heal underlying issues or reconsider if the goal truly aligns with your deepest values and purpose.

Embrace these three elements in harmony, and let them guide your journey of Pioneering Thinking, aligning your personal aspirations with the universal flow of energy, and steering your life towards fulfillment and enrichment.

Tapping Into the Wisdom of Your Inner Self

In the rich tapestry of Indian spirituality, akin to the profound teachings of the Upanishads, the concept of connecting with one's higher self is pivotal for effective and successful Pioneering Thinking. This inner connection is akin to attuning to Atman, the true essence within, which is a part of the universal Brahman.

1. **Understanding Your Spiritual Source**: Your inner spiritual source is an infinite reservoir of love, wisdom, and energy. This source might manifest in your consciousness as the Divine, Universal Consciousness, the Great Spirit, or simply your truest essence. It resides within you, as a part of your intrinsic being, waiting to be acknowledged and accessed.

2. **Higher Self as Your Inner Guide**: Imagine your higher self as a wise, enlightened version of you, residing within your own being. When in touch with this higher self, you feel a profound sense of clarity, empowerment, and understanding. It is this higher self that guides your journey, helping you to create experiences that are essential for your growth and learning.

3. **Recognizing the Connection**: You have undoubtedly experienced moments of connection with your higher self, though you may not have labeled them as such. Moments of feeling exceptionally clear, powerful, or deeply in love are instances where this connection becomes apparent. This connection can sometimes feel sporadic, but as you become more conscious of it, you can learn to tap into it more frequently and consistently.

4. **Developing a Two-Way Channel**: The link between your everyday personality and your higher self is a bidirectional channel. On one end, meditation and quiet introspection

open you up to receiving wisdom and guidance from your higher self. On the other, your active choices and willpowers channel this higher wisdom into your life, shaping your experiences.

5. **Receptive and Active Flow**: Cultivate a balance between being receptive to the guidance from your higher self and actively using this guidance to make conscious choices. In a receptive mode, seek answers through meditation and intuition. In an active mode, use this wisdom to make choices and visualize outcomes.

6. **Harmonious Co-creation**: When this channel is open and flowing in both directions, you find yourself guided by higher wisdom and actively co-creating your reality in alignment with this guidance. This process transforms your life into a journey of conscious creation, imbued with deeper meaning and purpose.

This practice of connecting with your higher self is not just a technique; it's a way of living that aligns you with the fundamental truths of existence. As you walk this path, let the ancient wisdom of India illuminate your journey, leading you to a life of deeper understanding, fulfillment, and harmonious co-creation with the universe.

Embracing Your Inner Spiritual Essence through Meditation

In the rich tapestry of Indian spirituality, akin to the profound insights of the Upanishads, meditation is a key to unlocking the experience of your spiritual core or higher self. As you delve into practices of relaxation, willpower, and empowerments, you gradually align yourself with this profound inner essence.

1. **Recognizing the Connection**: During your meditation, there may come moments of heightened awareness, a

feeling of a 'click' in your consciousness. This can manifest as a surge of energy or a warm, radiant sensation within you, signaling the awakening and flow of your inner spiritual energy.

2. **A Willpower Exercise to Connect with the Higher Self**:
   - Find a comfortable and quiet place to sit or lie down.
   - Allow your body and mind to relax deeply. Release all tension as you breathe slowly and deeply, sinking into a state of profound relaxation.
   - Envision a radiant light within your heart. Picture this light as warm, glowing, and loving. Imagine it expanding from your heart, growing brighter and more extensive, enveloping you in a luminous aura.
   - Visualize this light extending outward, transforming you into a golden sun, radiating loving energy to everything and everyone around you.
   - Affirm to yourself, with conviction and belief, "Divine light and divine love are flowing through me and radiating from me to all that surrounds me."
   - Repeat this affirmation, allowing its resonance to strengthen your sense of connection with your spiritual essence.
   - Optionally, incorporate other empowerments that resonate with your spirit, such as "The divine within me is shaping miracles in my life now" or "I am a conduit for creative energy and light."

3. **Deepening the Practice**: Regular practice of this exercise at the beginning of your meditation sessions can help deepen your connection with your higher self. This practice

is not just about willpower; it's an attunement to the deeper vibrations of your being.

4. **Personalization of Empowerments**: Feel free to modify or create empowerments that hold personal significance and power for you. The essence of this practice is to resonate with your inner truth and spiritual identity.

5. **Integration into Daily Life**: As you continue with this practice, you may notice an increased sense of serenity, clarity, and creativity in your daily life. These are signs of your growing alignment with your higher self.

This journey of connecting with your higher self through meditation is akin to the Indian spiritual pursuit of realizing the Atman, the innermost essence that is in union with Brahman, the universal spirit. As you explore and deepen this connection, you open yourself to a life of greater fulfillment, creativity, and spiritual harmony.

Embracing Life's Journey with Flexibility and Trust: An Indian Philosophical Perspective

In the diverse and profound landscape of Indian philosophy, the art of Pioneering Thinking resonates deeply with the ancient wisdom of 'Dharma' and 'Tao', emphasizing a harmonious and effortless alignment with the natural flow of life. This approach, akin to 'going with the flow', is a blend of clear intention and flexible surrender to the universe's rhythm.

1. **Effortless Flow Towards Goals**: The essence of this practice is akin to the concept of 'Wu Wei' in Taoism, often mirrored in Indian spiritual teachings. It suggests that you don't need to struggle or exert undue effort to achieve your goals. Instead, keep a clear vision of your destination while harmoniously flowing with life's currents. The path may sometimes appear indirect or divergent, but it often leads to

a more harmonious and effortless fulfillment of your aspirations.

2. **Holding Goals Lightly**: Embrace your goals with a gentle grasp, allowing space for adaptation and openness to new possibilities. This reflects the idea of 'Lila', the divine play, where life's journey is to be enjoyed, and destinations are flexible. Be firm in your vision but remain adaptable to life's ever-changing dynamics.

3. **Managing Emotional Attachments**: If intense emotions are tied to your goals, it's essential to address these feelings. An over-attachment can create fear of loss, inadvertently focusing energy on the absence rather than the manifestation of your desires. In such cases, work on cultivating inner security and confidence.

4. **Empowerments for Trust and Surrender**: To aid in this journey, empowerments rooted in trust and surrender can be powerful. They might include:

    - "The universe unfolds in perfect harmony; I embrace its flow."
    - "I release my grip and trust in the natural course of life."
    - "I am supported and guided in my journey, effortlessly."
    - "Abundance and love are inherent within me."
    - "I am a vessel of love and strength; the universe conspires in my favor."
    - "In my surrender, I find strength and guidance."

5. **Facing Fears and Cultivating Trust**: Explore and confront any fears associated with unmet goals. Understand that often, the journey towards a goal is as enriching as the

achievement itself. Empowerments such as "I am guided by divine love and wisdom" or "I trust in the generosity of the universe" can reinforce a sense of security and trust.

6. **Embracing the Journey**: The Indian spiritual path emphasizes the journey itself over the destination. Each moment and experience is part of a larger cosmic dance, where our individual paths are intricately woven into the tapestry of life.

Incorporating these principles into the practice of Pioneering Thinking not only enriches your personal aspirations but aligns them with the universal flow of energy and consciousness. This alignment fosters a life of fulfillment, serenity, and a deep connection with the cosmos.

Navigating Life's Journey with Intuition and Self-Discovery: A Reflection from Indian Wisdom

In the realm of Indian philosophy, there's a profound understanding that life is a journey of self-discovery, guided by inner wisdom and a surrender to the cosmic flow. This perspective aligns closely with the practice of Pioneering Thinking, emphasizing the need for introspection and alignment with one's true desires and life path.

1. **Understanding Emotional Attachments in Willpower**: When embarking on Pioneering Thinking, it's common to have deep-seated emotional attachments to certain goals. However, if these goals stem from fear or apprehension, it may be a signal to pause and introspect. This mirrors the Indian concept of 'Sankalpa', a heartfelt intention aligned with one's deeper aspirations, free from fear and conflict.

2. **The Role of Clearing Processes**: In Indian practices like Yoga and Ayurveda, clearing mental and emotional obstacles is essential for personal growth. Similarly, in

Pioneering Thinking, addressing internal conflicts and fears is crucial for manifesting your true aspirations. This process can be aided by various techniques and insightful readings that resonate with Indian philosophical teachings.

3. **Acceptance and Self-Exploration**: Sometimes, the inability to visualize a specific goal effectively might indicate a need to re-evaluate your true desires. This reflects the Indian tradition of self-inquiry ('Atma Vichara'), where introspection leads to a deeper understanding of one's true nature and desires.

4. **Aligning with the Higher Self**: Indian spiritual practices emphasize connecting with the 'Atman', or higher self. When practicing Pioneering Thinking, if you sense resistance or force, it's beneficial to consult your inner wisdom. This aligns with the Indian teaching that true knowledge and direction come from within.

5. **Embracing Life's Unfoldment**: Indian spirituality teaches that life is 'Leela', a divine play, where every experience is an opportunity for growth. If a willpower doesn't manifest as expected, it might be life's way of steering you towards something more suited to your true path. This idea is beautifully illustrated in the story of the individual who shifted from aspiring to be a comedian to finding fulfillment in being a minister, psychotherapist, and talk show host. This transition showcases how an apparent setback in willpower can lead to discovering a path more aligned with one's innate talents and purpose.

6. **Staying Open to New Directions**: Indian wisdom teaches the importance of remaining open and flexible to life's possibilities. Sometimes, what we initially desire may evolve or transform as we grow and learn more about ourselves.

In conclusion, the practice of Pioneering Thinking, when approached with the wisdom of Indian philosophy, becomes a journey of aligning with one's true desires, understanding the deeper self, and gracefully flowing with the universe's guidance. This approach not only aids in manifesting goals but also in discovering and fulfilling one's dharma or true purpose in life.

Cultivating a Mindset of Abundance: Insights from Indian Philosophy

In the rich tapestry of Indian philosophy, there's an inherent understanding of the universe's boundless generosity. This perspective aligns with the concept of Pioneering Thinking, particularly in manifesting prosperity. It's about embracing an abundance mindset, recognizing that the cosmos is replete with opportunities and resources for fulfillment and growth.

1. **The Principle of Abundance**: Indian philosophy, much like the concept of Pioneering Thinking, teaches that the universe is abundant and nurturing. The ancient scriptures, like the Vedas and Upanishads, speak of 'Aishwarya', the universal wealth that is available to all. It suggests that life, in its essence, is about experiencing and sharing this abundance.

2. **Challenging the Scarcity Mindset**: Often, cultural or societal conditioning instills a belief in scarcity, echoing sentiments like "resources are limited" or "life is inherently struggle". These beliefs, akin to what is termed 'scarcity programming' in willpower practices, contradict the Indian view of 'Lakshmi' – the goddess of wealth, who symbolizes the endless flow of prosperity and fortune.

3. **Redefining Prosperity**: In Indian thought, prosperity ('Samriddhi') isn't limited to material wealth. It

encompasses a holistic wealth – physical, emotional, spiritual, and intellectual. This aligns with the idea of seeking prosperity through Pioneering Thinking, where the goal isn't just material gain but a harmonious, enriched existence.

4. **Breaking Free from Limiting Beliefs**: Similar to overcoming scarcity programming, Indian spirituality encourages the shedding of limiting beliefs. Practices like 'Sankalpa' (positive intention-setting) and 'Dhyana' (meditation) are tools to transform one's mindset from scarcity to abundance.

5. **The Universal Right to Prosperity**: Contrary to beliefs that glorify poverty in the name of spirituality, Indian philosophy asserts that every individual has the right to prosperity. The concept of 'Dharma' emphasizes a balanced life where material and spiritual wealth coexist, supporting one's journey towards 'Moksha' (liberation).

6. **Collective Prosperity and Responsibility**: The Indian ethos of 'Vasudhaiva Kutumbakam' – the world is one family, highlights collective prosperity. It's not just about individual gain but ensuring that abundance flows to all, resonating with the notion that the universe's wealth is sufficient for everyone if shared wisely.

7. **Manifesting through Gratitude and Generosity**: Gratitude ('Kritajna') is a central theme in Indian culture, where acknowledging and appreciating the universe's gifts is crucial. This attitude, coupled with 'Dana' (the act of giving), reinforces the flow of prosperity in one's life, similar to the principles of Pioneering Thinking.

In essence, adopting a mindset of abundance and prosperity, inspired by Indian wisdom, involves recognizing the universe's infinite capacity to provide, believing in one's right to receive and share this abundance, and engaging in practices that affirm this belief, thereby creating a reality of plenitude and fulfillment.

Embracing Abundance in the Contemporary World: An Indian Perspective

In today's era, humanity appears to have drifted away from its intrinsic state of affluence. We've collectively sculpted a world imbalanced, where a minority basks in excessive riches, depleting natural reserves swiftly, while the majority endure scarcity. This reality is our collective creation, but it's within our power to transform it by reshaping our thoughts and lifestyles. We need to rediscover joy in life's simple pleasures. For many, especially in industrialized nations, this means adopting a lifestyle that's simpler, more attuned to nature. True abundance extends beyond material excess; it's about fulfilling our creative potential and establishing a harmony in giving and receiving.

This Earth is innately benevolent, rich, and nurturing. The only "evil," stemming from ignorance, is akin to a shadow - devoid of substance, simply an absence of enlightenment. You cannot dissipate a shadow through confrontation or resistance. It vanishes only when illuminated.

Reflect on your beliefs. Are they hindering your prosperity? Can you genuinely envision yourself as successful, content, and fulfilled? Can you open your eyes to the surrounding opulence and beauty? Can you imagine a world where everyone thrives?

Believing that the world can be a nurturing space for all is essential for personal success. Our innate loving nature means we naturally resist personal gain at the expense of others. Understanding that our personal fulfillment contributes to global happiness and empowers others to find their own joy is crucial.

To manifest prosperity, envision yourself living as you desire, engaged in work you love, content with your achievements, all within a world where others are equally fulfilled.

Here's an exercise to stimulate your imagination and broaden your willpower of true prosperity:

1. **Sit in a quiet space**: Find a calm environment, free of distractions. Sit comfortably, close your eyes, and take deep breaths. Let go of any immediate concerns or stress.

2. **Envision a world of balance**: Imagine a world where resources are used wisely and sustainably. Visualize communities living in harmony with nature, where the gap between the rich and the poor is significantly reduced.

3. **See yourself in this world**: Imagine your life in this balanced world. What are you doing? Picture yourself engaged in work that is not only fulfilling but also contributes positively to the world.

4. **Feel the satisfaction**: Immerse yourself in the feelings of contentment and joy that come from living a life of purpose and balance. Feel the gratitude for the abundance around you.

5. **Expand your vision**: Extend this vision to include others. Imagine people around the world finding their own paths to fulfillment and prosperity. Visualize a global community where each individual's success adds to the collective well-being.

6. **Return with a sense of purpose**: Gently bring yourself back to the present. Retain this feeling of possibility and purpose. Let this vision guide your actions and interactions.

This exercise is not just about personal prosperity but about contributing to a world where abundance is a shared experience, resonating deeply with the Indian ethos of 'Sarve Bhavantu Sukhinah' (May all beings be happy).

Willpower of Plentiful Harmony: A Guided Journey Through India's Essence

Envision a serene escape, comfortably nestled, your body and mind in a state of complete relaxation. Picture yourself amidst the lush landscapes of India - perhaps beside the verdant plains of Punjab or on the sun-kissed beaches of Goa. Take a moment to absorb the vivid details of these settings, feeling the joy and gratitude for the beauty around you.

Begin a journey of exploration. Visualize yourself wandering through the sprawling wheat fields of the Ganges plain or swimming in the tranquil waters of Dal Lake in Kashmir. With each step, discover diverse landscapes, from the majestic Himalayan peaks to the vast Thar Desert. Savor the uniqueness and beauty of each place, letting your imagination roam freely.

Now, transition to envisaging a return to a space that feels like home. Imagine a dwelling that resonates with simplicity yet radiates comfort and beauty, perhaps a traditional Indian bungalow surrounded by a lush garden. Visualize being surrounded by a loving family, a circle of friends, and a supportive community that celebrates the richness of Indian culture and tradition.

In this willpower, see yourself engaged in work that ignites your passion. Whether it's teaching, creating art, or contributing to the community, feel the satisfaction and joy it brings. Visualize appreciation from others and the rewards of your efforts, not just in monetary terms but as a deep, fulfilling contentment.

Expand this vision to encompass a world where individuals thrive in simplicity and abundance. Picture communities living in harmony, where the success of one adds to the well-being of all. Envision a world where people honor and cherish their connections with each other and with nature, reflecting the Indian ethos of Vasudhaiva Kutumbakam - the world is one family.

As you conclude this meditation, hold on to the sense of fulfillment and joy, and carry this vision into your daily life, embodying the principles of simplicity, abundance, and harmony in your actions and interactions.

Empowerments for Prosperity Rooted in Indian Ethos

1. "In simplicity lies great wealth. I embrace prosperity in its most elemental form."

2. "The universe, in its boundless generosity, offers abundance for all. I am part of this universal bounty."

3. "Abundance is the rhythm of my spirit, my natural state of being. I welcome it with open arms and a joyful heart."

4. "The Divine, the infinite source of all, generously provides for my every need."

5. "Happiness and prosperity are my birthright. I claim them now with gratitude and joy."

6. "As I flourish, I am a conduit of abundance, sharing my wealth with the world."

7. "I am open to the myriad joys and riches that life generously offers."

8. "I envision a world flourishing in abundance, where prosperity is shared by all."

9. "Financial success flows to me effortlessly, enriching my life."

10. "I revel in my financial prosperity, enjoying the wealth I have attained."

11. "Life's dance is meant to be joyful. I wholeheartedly embrace its pleasures and riches."

12. "I am a manifestation of prosperity, both in thought and reality."

13. "My financial resources abundantly fulfill my family's needs and my own."

14. "I joyfully earn ₹_____ every month, finding deep satisfaction in my financial stability."

15. "My financial circumstances fill me with deep contentment and joy."

16. "I am a reservoir of wealth, both materially and spiritually, experiencing abundance in its fullest form."

In the spirit of Indian wisdom, let these empowerments be a bridge to a life of richness, contentment, and sharing, inspired by ancient teachings and the timeless principles of the Upanishads.

Embracing Your Divine Essence: A Journey to Self-Acceptance

To harness the power of Pioneering Thinking in shaping our lives, it's essential to embrace the blessings life offers - our "good." Often, this is hindered by a deep-rooted sense of unworthiness that many of us carry from early life experiences. This sentiment usually stems from a belief that whispers, "I'm not worthy enough to receive life's gifts."

This inner conflict can manifest as a challenge in visualizing oneself in ideal circumstances, accompanied by doubts like, "Such blessings aren't meant for me," or "That's too good to be true for someone like me." If these thoughts resonate with you, it might be enlightening to explore your self-perception.

Your self-perception is your personal narrative about who you are. It's a complex mix of self-images and feelings about your worth. To unravel this, regularly ask yourself, "How do I perceive myself in this moment?" Notice how your self-image shifts throughout the day and across different contexts.

One profound exercise is to confront your physical self-perception. Ask, "How do I view my physical self right now?" Negative self-images, such as feeling unattractive, overweight, underweight, or generally inadequate, often signal an underlying struggle with self-love and acceptance.

It's surprising how many individuals, despite their outward charm and attractiveness, internally battle with feelings of inadequacy and undesirability. This internal conflict acts as a barrier, preventing them from realizing that they deserve the very best in life.

In Indian philosophy, the Upanishads teach us that the divine essence is within each individual. Recognizing this divine essence in ourselves can be a transformative experience, leading to a profound sense of worthiness and an openness to life's abundant gifts.

Embrace your divine essence. Recognize that you are deserving of all the wonders that life has to offer. By accepting and loving yourself fully, you open the doors to the infinite possibilities that life holds for you.

Embracing Self-Love Through Empowerments and Willpower

The transformative journey of self-improvement and self-love can be significantly enhanced through the practices of empowerments and Pioneering Thinking. These methods offer a pathway to rekindle a more loving, accepting self-perception. Recognizing areas where self-love lacks is the first step towards nurturing a more positive self-dialogue.

Start by identifying moments when you are overly critical or harsh towards yourself. Shift this narrative towards kindness and appreciation, much like you would do for a dear friend. This not only helps in self-growth but also in extending that love to others.

Reflect on the attributes you genuinely admire about yourself. Embrace your uniqueness, talents, and qualities, acknowledging that, like everyone, you are on a journey of growth and self-improvement. Express this self-appreciation through empowerments that resonate with your spirit. Examples include:

- "I am worthy of love and kindness."
- "My talents and creativity are valuable and unique."
- "I am deserving of happiness and success in my life."
- "I am attractive and radiate positivity."
- "The universe appreciates my existence and contributions."

Personalize these empowerments by addressing yourself directly, using your name, which can have a powerful, affirming impact:

- "Rahul, you are incredibly capable and smart."
- "Anjali, your warmth and compassion light up the room."

This method is particularly effective as it mirrors the nurturing and affirming words we yearned to hear in our formative years. It's a process of re-parenting oneself, offering the love, recognition, and validation that every individual deserves.

Lastly, visualize yourself in a state of joy, success, and fulfillment. Imagine scenarios where you are thriving, surrounded by love and appreciation. This practice not only enhances self-esteem but also aligns your energy with the positive outcomes you wish to manifest.

Remember, the journey to self-love is ongoing. Each affirmation, each moment of self-recognition is a step towards a more fulfilling and joyful life.

Fostering Self-Esteem and Embracing Universal Abundance through Willpower and Empowerments

The power of Pioneering Thinking and empowerments can be pivotal in reshaping perceptions about physical attributes and enhancing overall self-worth. For instance, if you're grappling with issues like weight management, a dual approach can be highly beneficial:

1. **Self-Acceptance and Affirmation:** Begin by cultivating love and acceptance for your current self. Utilize empowerments to reinforce your self-worth and beauty, irrespective of physical attributes.

2. **Positive Willpower and Goal Setting:** Concurrently, engage in visualizing your ideal physical state. Picture yourself healthy, energetic, and thriving. Empowerments in this context should focus on your journey towards this envisioned state.

This dual approach is effective for a variety of personal improvement goals. It's essential to remember that every day presents a fresh opportunity to embrace and celebrate your unique self.

Moreover, embracing the generosity of the universe and its willingness to fulfill your needs is a key aspect of this practice. Empowerments that open your heart to universal benevolence can significantly enhance your receptiveness to life's gifts:

- "I am a conduit for the universe's endless generosity. All forms of goodness naturally flow towards me."
- "I am deserving of abundance in all its forms - be it love, wealth, creativity, or health."
- "With gratitude, I accept the universe's gifts. My acceptance amplifies my ability to give."
- "The best of the universe is drawn to me, enriching my life in myriad ways."

To deepen these empowerments, try this guided meditation:

Self-Esteem and Universal Abundance Meditation:

1. **Relax and Center:** Find a quiet, comfortable space. Close your eyes and take deep, steady breaths. Feel each breath relaxing and centering your mind and body.

2. **Self-Acceptance Willpower:** Picture yourself in a serene, natural setting - perhaps a lush garden or beside a tranquil lake. See yourself in your current state, surrounded by a warm, golden light. This light represents unconditional love and acceptance. Feel it enveloping you, affirming your worthiness just as you are.

3. **Ideal Self Willpower:** Now, allow the image to transform gently into your ideal self – this could be a healthier, more energetic version of you. See yourself moving with ease,

glowing with health. Hold this image, feeling the reality of it in your heart.

4. **Receiving Universal Abundance:** Visualize a gentle shower of light descending from the sky, symbolizing the universe's abundance. As this light touches you, feel it bringing all that you desire – health, happiness, love. Affirm silently, "I openly receive the universe's gifts, and with gratitude, I flourish."

5. **Closing with Gratitude:** As your meditation concludes, take a moment to express silent thanks to the universe for its endless generosity. Slowly bring your awareness back to the present.

Integrate these practices into your daily routine, and observe as your self-esteem blossoms and your life becomes a reflection of the universe's bountiful nature.

Cultivating Self-Love and Recognition: A Guided Willpower and Empowerments

Embark on a journey of self-appreciation and recognition with this guided meditation, coupled with empowerments tailored to the Indian context, integrating wisdom from ancient philosophies and contemporary insights.

Self-Love Parade Willpower:

1. **Begin with a Common Scene:** Visualize yourself in a familiar setting, perhaps a bustling Indian bazaar, a tranquil park, or amidst the daily hustle of your city.

2. **Recognition from an Acquaintance:** In this scene, imagine encountering someone you know, or even a stranger, who looks at you with profound love and respect. Hear them express their admiration for a quality they truly appreciate in you.

3. **Growing Admiration:** Gradually, visualize more people joining in, echoing similar sentiments of appreciation and admiration. Feel their genuine respect for you.

4. **A Gathering of Adoration:** Envision this small group expanding into a crowd, each person gazing at you with admiration. Feel their respect and love, as if you were a respected leader or a beloved celebrity.

5. **A Celebration of You:** Imagine this turning into a grand parade or a stage event, with throngs of people cheering and applauding just for you. Listen to the roar of applause, the traditional Indian music playing, celebrating your essence.

6. **Acknowledge and Thank:** As you stand there, bask in the love and admiration, take a bow or join your hands in a Namaste, expressing gratitude for this overwhelming appreciation.

Empowerments for Self-Appreciation:

- "I embrace myself wholly, with all my unique qualities and imperfections. I am a perfect creation of the cosmos."

- "In my presence, I need not seek validation. My self-approval is my strength."

- "In the company of others, I stand tall and proud, a reflection of my self-love."

- "My voice and thoughts are a flow of creativity, deserving of being heard and cherished."

- "I am an embodiment of Shakti – powerful, loving, and full of creative life force."

Additional Resources:

For deeper exploration into self-awareness and introspection from Indian perspectives, consider the following books and resources:

1. **"The Power of Now" by Eckhart Tolle**: This book delves into mindfulness and the importance of living in the present moment, drawing parallels with concepts from Indian spiritual traditions like Advaita Vedanta.

2. **"Autobiography of a Yogi" by Paramahansa Yogananda**: Offering insights into the spiritual journey and self-realization, this classic book showcases the teachings of Yoga and meditation from an Indian perspective.

3. **"The Bhagavad Gita"**: Often referred to as the "song of the divine," this ancient Indian scripture offers profound wisdom on self-awareness, duty, and spiritual growth.

4. **"Mindfulness in Plain English" by Bhante Henepola Gunaratana**: This book provides a practical guide to mindfulness meditation, rooted in Buddhist teachings but with resonances in Indian spiritual practices.

5. **"The Yoga Sutras of Patanjali"**: Translated by various authors, including Swami Satchidananda and B.K.S. Iyengar, this text outlines the principles and practices of yoga, including self-awareness and mental discipline.

6. **"Ayurveda: The Science of Self-Healing" by Dr. Vasant Lad**: Exploring the holistic healing system of Ayurveda, this book offers insights into achieving physical, mental, and emotional balance through diet, lifestyle, and herbal remedies.

7. **"Inner Engineering: A Yogi's Guide to Joy" by Sadhguru**: In this book, Sadhguru, a renowned Indian yogi and mystic, offers practical tools and insights for inner transformation and self-discovery.

Additionally, for a blend of modern therapeutic techniques with Indian traditions like Yoga and Ayurveda, you may explore holistic wellness centers or retreats led by experienced practitioners who integrate these approaches for comprehensive well-being.

Cultivating Generosity: Embracing the Flow of Life's Energy

In the rich tapestry of Indian culture, where ancient wisdom meets modern insights, lies a profound understanding of the universe's nature as a constant flow of energy. This flow, akin to the eternal rivers of India, symbolizes the essence of giving and receiving, a concept deeply rooted in our traditions and daily lives.

The Principle of Generosity:

1. **Understanding the Universe's Rhythm:** Recognize the universe as an entity of dynamic energy, where change and fluidity are inherent. Like the Ganges flowing endlessly, life too is in perpetual motion.

2. **Embracing the Cycle of Giving and Receiving:** In the spirit of the timeless Indian ethos of 'Karma' and

'Dharma', engage in the act of giving. As we give, we align ourselves with the universe's rhythm, creating a vacuum for more abundance.

3. **Overcoming the Fear of Scarcity:** Let go of the fear-driven belief that resources are limited. This fear, often rooted in insecurity, blocks the natural flow of energy and abundance in our lives.

4. **The Many Forms of Energy:** Energy manifests in myriad forms, such as love, recognition, wealth, and companionship. The principle of outflowing applies to all these forms, much like the diverse expressions of Indian culture.

5. **Observing the Effects of Hoarding:** Notice that those who cling tightly to what they have, often driven by a sense of deprivation, are usually the ones who feel most unfulfilled. This is akin to holding the waters of a river – the tighter the grip, the less they can hold.

Applying the Principle in Daily Life:

1. **Cultivate a Generous Spirit:** Embrace the joy of giving. Share warmth, compassion, and resources selflessly, reflecting the ethos of Indian hospitality and generosity.

2. **Trust in the Universe's Abundance:** Believe in the abundant nature of the universe, a belief deeply embedded in Indian spirituality. Trust that the universe will provide and replenish what you give.

3. **Release and Let Flow:** Practicing yoga and meditation can be instrumental in letting go of possessiveness. These ancient Indian practices teach us to release our grasp and allow life's energy to flow freely.

4. **Balance in All Things:** Just as the Indian philosophy of 'Middle Path' suggests, find a balance in giving and receiving. Neither hoard nor squander, but maintain a harmonious flow.
5. **Observe Nature's Generosity:** Take inspiration from the natural world around us. Observe how trees give shade and fruit, rivers nourish lands, and the sun gives its warmth unconditionally, embodying the essence of outflowing.

By embracing this principle of outflowing, we align ourselves with the universe's natural flow, opening our lives to a richer, more fulfilling experience, deeply rooted in the wisdom of Indian culture and spirituality.

Embracing the Joy of Generosity: The Essence of Sharing in Indian Philosophy

In the rich tapestry of Indian wisdom, where ancient Vedas meet the rhythm of modern life, there exists a profound understanding of the joy of generosity. This concept, deeply ingrained in Indian culture, speaks to the heart of human existence — the art of giving not out of obligation, but from a place of sheer delight and self-fulfillment.

Understanding the True Nature of Giving:

1. **Discovering the Inner Source of Joy:** In the Indian context, joy is often equated with the inner Ananda — a state of bliss. Realize that happiness is an internal state, abundant and self-replenishing, waiting to be shared.
2. **The Pleasure of Sharing:** True generosity is not a sacrifice or a duty but a joyful act. This aligns with the Indian tradition of 'Seva' – selfless service – where the act of giving itself brings happiness.

3. **The Infinite Reservoir of Love:** Indian teachings often emphasize that we are beings of love. This infinite source within us needs to be tapped and shared, reflecting the essence of Bhakti (devotion).
4. **Reversing the Flow:** When we give genuinely, we shift from seeking external validation to experiencing internal satisfaction. This shift mirrors the Indian principle of Karma — what we give, we receive.

Practical Ways to Cultivate Generosity:

1. **Giving as a Natural Act:** Embrace giving as an enjoyable and natural part of life. Let it arise spontaneously, much like the Indian festival of giving, Daan Utsav, where sharing is a celebration.
2. **Balanced Giving and Receiving:** Recognize that a healthy flow of energy involves both giving and receiving. In the Indian ethos, this balance is crucial for sustaining the universal cycle of life.
3. **Saying No When Necessary:** Understand that true giving also means setting boundaries. The Indian concept of Dharma emphasizes that righteousness includes respecting oneself and others.
4. **Self-Care is Essential:** Remember, giving to oneself is as important as giving to others. The ancient Indian practice of Ayurveda teaches self-care as a precursor to caring for others.
5. **Sharing Beyond Material Wealth:** Expand the concept of giving to include sharing knowledge, wisdom, and emotional support, reflecting the Indian tradition of Guru-Shishya (teacher-student) relationship.

The Impact of Generosity:

1. **Creating a Ripple Effect:** As you give, you inspire others to give, creating a ripple effect. This reflects the Indian belief in Vasudhaiva Kutumbakam — the world is one family.

2. **Fostering Community and Connection:** Generosity strengthens community bonds, resonating with the Indian value of community living where sharing and caring are inherent.

3. **Experiencing Inner Fulfillment:** The act of giving aligns with the Indian pursuit of inner peace and contentment, as outlined in the Upanishads and other ancient scriptures.

By embracing the joy of giving and understanding its deep-rooted place in Indian philosophy and way of life, we open ourselves to a world of abundance and happiness. This approach to life transforms not just the individual, but the collective consciousness, steering us towards a more empathetic and connected world.

Embracing the Flow of Generosity: Cultivating the Art of Giving in the Indian Ethos

In the vibrant mosaic of Indian culture, where ancient traditions harmonize with contemporary life, lies a deep-rooted belief in the power of generosity. This principle, embedded in Indian philosophy, underscores the art of giving, not merely as a duty but as a fulfilling and joyful practice.

Cultivating the Art of Giving:

1. **Expressing Gratitude and Appreciation:** Make it a habit to convey your gratitude to others in diverse ways. Perhaps, write a heartfelt letter or offer a sincere compliment. In Indian culture, expressions of gratitude are often

accompanied by small tokens of appreciation, like sweets or flowers, to reinforce the sentiment.

2. **Sharing Personal Belongings:** Peruse through your belongings and gift items that are less used to those who might cherish them. This practice reflects the Indian tradition of 'Daan' (charity), where giving away belongings is seen as an act of virtue.

3. **Conscious Spending:** Experiment with spending a little more for quality or joy, not just for oneself but for others too. This could mean buying a friend a cup of chai or donating to a local cause. Such acts resonate with the Indian concept of 'Lakshmi', the goddess of wealth, who is believed to favor those who are not just receivers but givers as well.

4. **Tithing:** Adopt the practice of tithing, an ancient concept also found in Indian spirituality, where a portion of your earnings is offered to spiritual or charitable causes, acknowledging the cyclical flow of abundance.

5. **Creative Outflowing:** Innovate new ways to share your energy and resources. This could be volunteering your time, sharing your skills, or even simple acts of kindness. The Indian epic, Mahabharata, illustrates numerous instances where heroes are celebrated for their generosity and creative ways of giving.

The Impact of Generosity:

1. **Creating Positive Ripple Effects:** Your acts of generosity can inspire and influence others, creating a community where giving becomes a natural way of life.

2. **Fulfilling Personal Growth:** Giving generously can lead to a sense of personal fulfillment and happiness, reflecting

the Indian belief in 'Karma Yoga' - the yoga of selfless action.

3. **Balanced Living:** Generosity should also extend to oneself, ensuring a balance between giving and receiving, much like the Indian concept of 'Dharma' which advocates a life of balance and harmony.

4. **Cultural Integration:** Integrating these practices into your daily life not only enriches your personal experience but also contributes to preserving and promoting the rich cultural heritage of India.

In essence, the art of giving, deeply interwoven into the Indian fabric of life, is a practice that extends beyond material gifts. It is about sharing love, kindness, and compassion, creating a world where generosity flows freely, enriching both giver and receiver. This approach to life transforms not just the individual, but also the collective consciousness, steering us towards a more empathetic and connected world.

Harnessing the Power of Mind for Holistic Healing: Integrating Pioneering Thinking in Indian Wellness Practices

In the intricate tapestry of Indian wellness philosophies, where the alignment of body, mind, and spirit forms the cornerstone of health, the practice of Pioneering Thinking emerges as a vital tool for holistic healing. Rooted in the ancient wisdom of Ayurveda and Yoga, and resonating with the principles of modern holistic health, this technique underscores the interconnectedness of our physical, emotional, mental, and spiritual well-being.

Understanding Holistic Health through Pioneering Thinking:

1. **The Unity of Being:** Acknowledge that physical ailments often mirror internal imbalances. In Ayurvedic tradition, health is seen as a harmony of body ('Sharira'), mind ('Manas'), and soul ('Atma'). Visualize this triad in balance to foster overall well-being.

2. **Mind-Body Communication:** Utilize Pioneering Thinking as a bridge between mind and body. This aligns with the Indian belief in 'Prana', the life force, which can be directed through focused intent, influencing our physical health.

3. **Restoring Harmony:** Recognize that illness can be a message urging introspection and realignment. In Yoga, this is akin to understanding 'Kleshas', or afflictions. Use willpower to address and soothe these inner conflicts.

Practical Steps for Healing Through Willpower:

1. **Imagery for Healing:** Imagine your body healing, using symbols and images that resonate with you. For instance, envision a bright light enveloping an ailing part, restoring its vitality, a practice reminiscent of 'Pranic' healing techniques.

2. **Empowerments for Well-being:** Pair willpower with positive empowerments in Sanskrit or your preferred language. For instance, "Arogyam Dhanasampada" (Health is Wealth), to reinforce the healing process.

3. **Integrating Ayurvedic Principles:** Align your willpower practices with Ayurvedic concepts like balancing 'Doshas' (body elements) and cleansing 'Nadis' (energy channels).

4. **Yogic Breathing and Willpower:** Combine 'Pranayama' (breath control) with willpower for deeper impact. Visualize healing energy flowing with each breath, rejuvenating your body and mind.
5. **Incorporating Meditation:** Use 'Dhyana' (meditation) to deepen your willpower practice, enhancing mental clarity and focus, crucial for effective healing.

Embracing Traditional Wisdom and Modern Insights:

1. **Incorporate Upanishadic Insights:** Draw from the profound wisdom of the Upanishads, visualizing the unity of 'Atman' (soul) and 'Brahman' (universal consciousness) for spiritual healing.
2. **Leverage Technology:** Utilize modern meditation and willpower apps that blend ancient wisdom with contemporary science, providing guided imagery tailored to healing.
3. **Seek Guidance:** Consider consulting Ayurvedic practitioners or Yoga therapists who can guide personalized willpower techniques suited to your unique constitution.
4. **Nurture Community Healing:** Share willpower practices within community settings, drawing inspiration from Indian 'Satsangs' or gatherings, fostering collective healing.

In essence, integrating Pioneering Thinking into the rich fabric of Indian wellness practices not only nurtures individual health but also contributes to the preservation and evolution of ancient wisdom. This holistic approach, blending traditional insights and modern techniques, paves the way for a journey towards a balanced, healthy, and harmonious life.

Embracing Wholeness: Understanding the Holistic Message of Illness in the Indian Context

In the rich tapestry of Indian philosophy, where the harmony of body, mind, and spirit is deeply rooted, the interpretation of illness transcends mere physical ailment. It is often viewed as a confluence of emotional, mental, spiritual, and physical elements, reflecting a profound understanding similar to Ayurveda's holistic approach. This perspective invites us to explore deeper into our consciousness, recognizing illness as a meaningful dialogue between our inner selves and our external expressions.

1. The Multi-Dimensional Nature of Illness:

- **Emotional Echoes:** Illness can mirror suppressed emotions. In the Indian tradition, this aligns with the concept of 'Chitta' (consciousness), where repressed feelings may manifest as physical symptoms.
- **Mental Patterns:** Like the repetitive chanting of a 'mantra', our mind's ingrained beliefs can shape our health. Patterns of thought, akin to 'Samskaras' in Yoga, play a crucial role in our wellbeing.

2. The Message Behind the Malady:

- **Signal for Self-Care:** Often, illness is a reminder from our body to pause and reconnect with our inner selves, akin to the practice of 'Svadhyaya' (self-study) in Yoga.
- **Opportunity for Alignment:** Like aligning 'Doshas' in Ayurveda, illness can signal a need for realigning our life's balance.

3. Transformative Approaches to Healing:

- **Mindful Meditation:** Embrace practices like 'Dhyana', visualizing healing energy restoring balance.
- **Emotional Release:** Acknowledge and release pent-up emotions, perhaps through practices akin to 'Bhakti Yoga', channeling emotional energy in a positive direction.

4. The Wisdom of Ancestral Patterns:

- **Understanding Genetic Narratives:** Like the continuity in 'Vedic' lineages, familial health patterns offer insights into our health predispositions.
- **Rewriting Health Scripts:** Use willpower and positive empowerments to break the cycle of inherited health issues.

5. Creating a Space for Healing:

- **Sacred Rest:** Embrace the recuperative power of rest, seeing it as a form of 'Tapas' (austerity) for rejuvenation.
- **Nurturing with Nature:** Incorporate elements of 'Prakriti' (nature) in healing, using natural remedies and aligning with the rhythms of nature.

6. Integrating Modern Insights and Ancient Wisdom:

- **Collaborative Healing:** Combine modern medical treatments with traditional practices for a holistic approach.
- **Technological Harmony:** Utilize technology for health monitoring while staying grounded in traditional wellness practices.

In conclusion, the Indian perspective encourages viewing illness not as a mere physical dysfunction but as a multifaceted message urging introspection and holistic rebalancing. This approach, blending ancient wisdom with modern understanding, offers a path to not just healing the ailment but nurturing the totality of our being.

Inner Healing: Embracing the Indian Ethos of Wellness

In the rich tapestry of Indian philosophy, where the emphasis is on the integration of mind, body, and spirit, the concept of healing transcends mere physical symptoms. This holistic view recognizes that true healing often originates from within, even as external treatments play a role. It's a journey deeply interwoven with our emotional, mental, and spiritual states, echoing the ancient principles of Ayurveda and Yoga.

1. The Inner Source of Healing:

- **Quietness and Connection:** Regular introspection and meditation, akin to 'Dhyana' in Yoga, can preempt the need for physical ailments to alert us to inner imbalances.
- **Messages in Maladies:** Like deciphering hidden messages in ancient scriptures, understanding the emotional and mental roots behind our illnesses can guide us to profound healing.

2. Listening to the Inner Self:

- **Introspective Guidance:** In moments of stillness, akin to the meditative silence in Indian temples, listen for the inner voice that guides toward healing.
- **External Support:** Sometimes, akin to seeking guidance from a 'Guru', assistance from therapists or healers can help illuminate the path to wellness.

3. Navigating Illness without Guilt:

- **Journey, not Judgment:** Viewing illness as a part of our life's journey, much like the 'Karma' we bear, without attaching guilt or blame.
- **Sickness as a Teacher:** Embracing illness as a teacher, a 'Guru', in the journey of life, offering lessons for growth and evolution.

4. Willpower for Healing:

- **Mental Imagery for Wellness:** Employing willpower techniques, akin to visualizing deities in meditation, to envisage complete healing and health.
- **Affirmative Mantras:** Using empowerments as positive mantras, reinforcing the belief in one's health and vitality.

5. Preventative Wellness:

- **Proactive Health Empowerments:** Regularly affirming and visualizing good health as a form of preventative care, much like daily 'Pranayama' for respiratory health.
- **Embracing Holistic Practices:** Incorporating a lifestyle that aligns with Ayurvedic principles for balanced living, preventing the onset of ailments.

6. Embracing Traditional Wisdom in Modern Healing:

- **Ancient Wisdom for Contemporary Cure:** Integrating the wisdom of Ayurveda and Yoga with modern medicine for a holistic approach to health.
- **Miraculous Recoveries through Mind-Body Harmony:** Acknowledging the power of mind-body harmony in healing serious illnesses, a concept deeply rooted in Indian wellness practices.

The Indian perspective on healing invites us to see physical ailments not just as bodily dysfunctions but as opportunities for deep introspection and spiritual growth. It encourages us to harness the power of our inner selves, blending ancient wisdom with contemporary understanding, to not only treat the symptoms but to nurture the whole being towards sustained health and vitality.

Inner Transformation: Tales of Healing and Wholeness from the Heart of India

In the profound wisdom of Indian philosophy, where the union of body, mind, and spirit is revered, stories abound of remarkable transformations and healings. These tales, passed down through generations, emphasize the power of the mind and the soul in overcoming physical adversities. They resonate with the ancient practices of Ayurveda and Yoga, where healing is as much about the inner journey as it is about physical recovery.

1. Miraculous Recoveries:

- **The Story of Resilience:** Drawing inspiration from a woman who, against all odds, overcame severe injuries from an accident, much like the legendary warriors of ancient Indian epics. Her journey of recovery, aided by willpower techniques and physical therapy, echoes the tales where mind conquers matter.

- **A Triumph Over Fate:** A man, much like a modern-day sage, turned to introspection upon facing a life-threatening diagnosis. His story of using willpower, along with medical care, leading to the disappearance of his tumor, mirrors the mystical healings often described in Indian lore.

2. The Power of Willpower:

- **Ancestral Wisdom in Modern Times:** These contemporary stories reflect the age-old Indian belief in the power of the mind and willpower, much like the 'Siddhis' described in ancient texts.

- **Complementing Conventional Medicine:** Just as Ayurveda and Yoga have traditionally complemented each other, willpower is seen as a vital supplement to modern medical treatments.

3. Embracing Life's Challenges:

- **Illness as a Teacher:** In Indian philosophy, every experience, including illness, is an opportunity for growth and learning. Some ailments may serve a deeper purpose in our lives, much like the challenges faced by heroes in Indian mythology, leading to profound spiritual and personal growth.

- **The Journey of the Soul:** Recognizing that some health challenges might be part of one's soul journey, reflecting the concept of 'Karma' and 'Dharma' in Indian spirituality.

4. The Final Transition:

- **Embracing Mortality:** In the Indian ethos, death is seen as a natural transition, an integral part of life's cycle, as depicted in texts like the Bhagavad Gita. The focus at life's end shifts to visualizing a peaceful and fulfilling conclusion, embracing the inevitable with grace and acceptance.

These stories and practices remind us of the timeless wisdom inherent in Indian culture – that healing is a journey of not just the body, but also the soul. It's a path of embracing challenges as opportunities for growth, using willpower as a powerful tool for healing, and ultimately, understanding life's transitory nature and accepting all its phases with equanimity and grace.

The Art of Distant Healing: Bridging Mind, Body, and Spirit

In the rich tapestry of Indian spiritual traditions, there is a deep-seated belief in the interconnectedness of all beings. This principle is vividly reflected in the practice of distant healing, a concept that transcends physical boundaries, tapping into the universal consciousness that binds us all. Rooted in ancient wisdom, yet echoing modern scientific inquiries into the power of intention and prayer, distant healing is a testament to the unseen forces that shape our reality.

1. Universal Connectedness in Healing:

- **The Principle of Oneness:** Just as the ancient Upanishads speak of the oneness of the universe, the practice of distant healing is based on the interconnected nature of all consciousness. By understanding this unity, one can channel healing energy to others.

- **The Power Beyond Distance:** Drawing from the teachings of great Indian sages, distant healing illustrates that physical distance is no barrier when it comes to affecting change in another's well-being.

2. Harnessing Inner Healing Power:

- **Channeling Universal Energy:** Emulating the yogic practice of harnessing universal prana, the healer visualizes themselves as a conduit for divine energy, directing it towards the person in need.

- **Visualizing Perfect Health:** The practice involves visualizing the recipient in their ideal state of health and happiness, reminiscent of the Indian belief in visualizing positive outcomes.

3. Respecting Individual Journeys:

- **Understanding Karmic Choices:** In line with the concept of karma, distant healing acknowledges that each individual's journey, including their health, is part of their soul's path. Healing is offered without attachment to the outcome.

- **Supporting Soul's Wisdom:** The healer's intention is to support the recipient's higher self in whatever healing process is needed, aligning with the Indian ethos of supporting one's Dharma.

4. Scientific Perspectives on Distant Healing:

- **Dr. Amit Goswami**: A quantum physicist and author, Dr. Goswami's books such as "The Quantum Doctor" and "Quantum Creativity" delve into the intersection of quantum physics, consciousness, and healing. He discusses how focused intention can influence health outcomes.

- **Dr. Deepak Chopra**: Renowned for his work in mind-body medicine, Dr. Chopra's books like "The Spontaneous Fulfillment of Desire" and "Ageless Body, Timeless Mind" explore the connection between consciousness, intention, and healing.

- **Dr. B. M. Hegde**: A cardiologist and author, Dr. Hegde's books such as "What Doctors Don't Get to Study in Medical School" and "Healing: The Quantum

Way" discuss holistic approaches to health and the role of consciousness in healing.

5. Personal Practices for Distant Healing:

- **Developing a Personal Method:** Inspired by Indian meditation techniques, one can create a personal healing ritual, incorporating elements like deep meditation, willpower of energy flow, and empowerments of health.

- **Respecting Free Will:** Just as the Indian spiritual path respects individual free will, distant healing is performed with the understanding that the recipient's higher self will accept the healing in the manner that is best for them.

In this practice, the ancient wisdom of India meets the frontiers of modern science, revealing the profound impact our thoughts and intentions can have on the world around us. Distant healing is not just a technique but a spiritual journey, emphasizing the unity of all existence and the power of love and intention to transcend physical limitations.

Part 3
The Essence of Inner Harmony: Meditations and Empowerments

Drawing inspiration from the rich spiritual heritage of India, we delve into the realm of meditations and empowerments, essential tools for inner harmony and self-realization. These practices, deeply rooted in the ancient wisdom of the Vedas and Upanishads, also reflect the cutting-edge insights of modern psychology and holistic health.

1. Meditation: The Path to Inner Silence

- **Mindfulness and Awareness:** Embrace the age-old practice of Dhyana, focusing on mindfulness and heightened awareness. This aligns with the teachings of great Indian sages who advocated for a deep connection with the self.

- **Breath and Energy Flow:** Incorporate Pranayama, the art of breath control, to channelize life energy (Prana), promoting mental clarity and physical wellbeing.

2. Empowerments: Words of Power

- **Positive Self-Talk:** Craft empowerments inspired by ancient Sanskrit mantras, embodying positivity and self-empowerment. This practice mirrors the traditional use of sound vibrations in Indian spirituality to influence consciousness.

- **Creating Reality:** Follow the wisdom of the Upanishads which state that thoughts create reality. Use empowerments to shape a reality filled with health, happiness, and prosperity.

3. Thematic Meditations for Holistic Wellbeing

- **Chakra Meditation:** Explore meditations focused on the seven Chakras, aligning them to enhance physical, emotional, and spiritual balance, drawing from the ancient Indian system of energy centers.

- **Nature-Inspired Meditation:** Practice meditation techniques that involve visualizing natural elements, a concept deeply ingrained in Indian spirituality, where nature is revered and seen as a source of life and energy.

4. The Power of Willpower

- **Guided Imagery:** Engage in willpower exercises that are akin to ancient Indian willpower practices used in Yoga and meditation, focusing on positive outcomes and desired life scenarios.

5. Incorporating Indian Philosophical Concepts

- **Non-Attachment and Detachment:** Integrate the teachings of the Bhagavad Gita about non-attachment into meditations and empowerments, focusing on the process rather than the outcome.

- **Dharma and Righteousness:** Create empowerments that encourage alignment with one's Dharma (duty or righteousness), reflecting the moral and ethical teachings of Indian philosophy.

6. Empowerments Aligned with Indian Wisdom

- **Harmony with the Universe:** Empowerments such as "I am in harmonious alignment with the generous flow of the universe," reflect the Indian ethos of cosmic harmony.

- **Inner Peace:** Use empowerments like "I embody the tranquility of the deep Indian oceans, calm and serene," to cultivate inner peace and stability.

7. Stories and Parables as Meditative Tools

- **Incorporate Indian Parables:** Use stories and parables from Indian epics and folklore as contemplative tools during meditation, providing deep insights and moral lessons.

8. Applying Modern Insights

- **Integrate Latest Findings:** Apply the latest psychological and neuroscientific findings to enhance the effectiveness of these age-old practices, blending tradition with modern understanding.

In this synthesis of meditative and affirmative practices, we see a beautiful confluence of India's spiritual legacy with contemporary thought. These practices offer a pathway to self-discovery and inner peace, encouraging us to live in harmony with ourselves and the world around us.

Your Words Shape Your Destiny: Wisdom from the Ages

In the ancient land of Bharat, where the wisdom of the Vedas and Upanishads has guided souls for centuries, there lies a profound understanding of the power of spoken words. Echoing this timeless wisdom, let's explore how our declarations shape our reality, much like the guiding principle found in the revered text of the Bhagavad Gita.

1. The Power of Sankalpa (Intention):

- **Ancient Insights:** Embrace the concept of Sankalpa from the Vedic traditions, where setting a strong intention is seen as the first step to manifesting one's desires.

- **Modern Interpretation:** In today's context, this translates to the power of positive empowerments and goal-setting, aligning with the latest psychological research on the impact of positive thinking.

2. The Luminescence of Your Path:

- **Guidance from the Rishis:** The wisdom of the ancient sages proclaims that the purity of one's speech and mind illuminates the path of life, echoing the teachings of the Upanishads.
- **Application in Daily Life:** Incorporate clear, positive empowerments in daily routines to illuminate your path towards personal and professional goals.

3. Manifesting Through Words:

- **Scriptural Foundations:** Drawing from the Upanishads, understand how the vibration of your words can influence the universe, much like the concept of Nada Brahma - the universe as sound.
- **Practical Use:** Use mantras and empowerments in your daily practice to create a resonant field that aligns with your aspirations.

4. Integrating Ancient Wisdom in Contemporary Life:

- **Balancing Tradition and Modernity:** Blend the ancient practices of mantra and affirmation with contemporary self-help strategies to create a holistic approach to personal growth.
- **Technological Support:** Utilize modern tools like meditation apps that offer guided empowerments, combining traditional wisdom with digital convenience.

5. Stories as Empowerments:

- **Mythological Examples:** Learn from Indian mythology, where characters speak their destiny into existence, serving as allegories for the power of empowerments.

- **Narrative as a Tool:** Use storytelling as a method to reinforce positive empowerments, drawing inspiration from Indian epics like the Mahabharata and Ramayana.

6. Empowerments for a Balanced Life:

- **Physical and Spiritual Well-Being:** Craft empowerments that promote not just material success but also spiritual peace, mirroring the Indian ethos of a balanced life.

- **Community and Individual Growth:** Create empowerments that nurture personal ambitions while contributing to the welfare of the community, reflecting the Indian ideal of 'Vasudhaiva Kutumbakam' (the world is one family).

Incorporating these practices into your life, guided by the timeless wisdom of ancient Indian philosophy and the universal truths found in the Upanishads, you can set forth empowerments that sculpt a luminous and enriching journey. As you articulate your aspirations, the cosmos harmonizes, illuminating the path ahead with clarity and divine purpose.

Harmonizing Energy: A Meditation Inspired by Indian Wisdom

In the spiritual landscape of India, where the balance between the cosmic and the earthly is deeply revered, let us explore a meditation technique that echoes this harmony. This practice, reminiscent of the ancient Indian practice of grounding and energy flow, aims to balance our inner energies with the rhythms of the universe.

1. Preparing for Meditation:

- **Position:** Sit comfortably, maintaining an upright posture, either in a chair or cross-legged on the floor, reminiscent of the traditional Indian meditation asanas.
- **Breath:** Begin with deep, slow breathing, reminiscent of Pranayama, focusing on the rhythmic inhalation and exhalation to reach a state of deep relaxation.

2. Establishing a Grounding Cord:

- **Willpower:** Imagine a cord, akin to the roots of the sacred Banyan tree, extending from the base of your spine deep into the Earth.
- **Connection to Earth:** Visualize the nurturing energy of Mother Earth (Bhumi), flowing up this cord, filling your body with stability and nourishment.

3. Invoking Cosmic Energy:

- **Celestial Flow:** Picture the vibrant, cosmic energy descending from the universe, entering through the crown of your head, akin to the divine blessings showered upon sages in the Indian epics.
- **Harmonious Confluence:** Envision the celestial energy merging seamlessly with the earthly energy within you, creating a balance that resonates with the concept of 'Loka Samastha Sukhino Bhavantu' (May all beings everywhere be happy).

4. The Dance of Energies:

- **Dynamic Flow:** Feel the dual energies dancing within you, one ascending from Earth, the other descending from the cosmos, meeting and mingling in a harmonious ballet.
- **Inner Harmony:** Embrace this union of energies, mirroring the balance of Shiva and Shakti, the cosmic dance of creation and destruction, maintaining equilibrium.

5. Integration and Completion:

- **Awareness:** Stay aware of this flow throughout the meditation, ensuring you remain grounded yet open to cosmic inspiration.
- **Gratitude:** Conclude your meditation with a moment of gratitude, thanking the Earth and the cosmos for their energies, reflecting the Indian tradition of expressing gratitude towards nature.

This meditation technique, deeply rooted in Indian spiritual traditions, helps maintain a sacred balance between the grounding energy of the Earth and the expansive energy of the cosmos. By regularly practicing this, you embrace an inner harmony that reflects the profound balance observed in the natural world around us.

Revitalizing Pranic Meditation: An Indian-Inspired Energy Center Activation

This meditation, inspired by the ancient Indian practices of Pranic healing and Chakra balancing, is a transformative exercise aimed at purifying and revitalizing your body's energy centers. It is particularly beneficial in the morning, as part of a meditative practice, or whenever you need rejuvenation.

1. Preparation:

- **Position:** Lie down on your back comfortably, either with your arms relaxed at your sides or with your hands gently resting on your abdomen, mirroring the relaxed posture in Yoga Nidra.
- **Breath:** Close your eyes and begin with deep, rhythmic breathing, reminiscent of Pranayama practices, to bring about a state of tranquility.

2. Crown Chakra (Sahasrara):

- **Willpower:** Imagine a radiant sphere of golden light at the crown of your head, symbolizing the Sahasrara Chakra.
- **Breath Focus:** Inhale and exhale slowly and deeply five times, focusing on the crown, feeling the light infuse your being with universal consciousness.

3. Throat Chakra (Vishuddha):

- **Golden Light:** Shift your attention to your throat area, visualizing a luminous golden sphere, embodying the Vishuddha Chakra, center of communication and creativity.
- **Breathing:** Breathe gently into this space five times, feeling the light expanding, enhancing your ability to express and communicate.

4. Heart Chakra (Anahata):

- **Heart Center:** Focus on the center of your chest, visualizing a glowing sphere of golden light at your heart, the Anahata Chakra, symbolizing love and compassion.

- **Breath and Expansion:** With five deep breaths, feel the energy of love and compassion radiating outwards, encompassing all beings.

5. Solar Plexus Chakra (Manipura):

- **Navel Focus:** Bring your awareness to your solar plexus or navel area, imagining a sphere of golden light, representing the Manipura Chakra, your center of power and confidence.
- **Energizing Breath:** Breathe deeply into this center five times, feeling a surge of energy and empowerment emanating from within.

This practice, steeped in the wisdom of Indian spiritual traditions, serves as a powerful tool for activating and balancing your Chakras. By channeling the life force or Prana through these centers, you awaken a deeper connection with your inner self, fostering harmony and vitality in your daily life.

Pranic Energy Circulation: An Indian-Inspired Vitalizing Meditation

This meditation is an amalgamation of traditional Indian pranic healing and chakra stimulation techniques, designed to revitalize and balance the body's energy system. Ideal for morning routines or any time you need a boost of vitality.

1. Preparation:

- **Posture:** Lie down in Shavasana, a relaxed but alert yogic posture, ensuring your back is straight and you're comfortable.
- **Breath:** Begin with deep, controlled breathing, reminiscent of Pranayama, to enter a state of relaxation.

2. Energy Centers Activation:

- **Pelvic Area (Svadhishthana Chakra):** Focus on your pelvic area, visualizing a golden sphere of light, representing the Svadhishthana Chakra. Inhale and exhale deeply five times, feeling the light's energy radiating.

- **Feet (Root Energy):** Shift attention to your feet, visualizing another glowing sphere, grounding your energy. Breathe into this area five times.

3. Full-Body Energy Synchronization:

- **Energy Alignment:** Imagine all energy centers (from head to feet) activated and glowing simultaneously, creating a harmonious alignment, like radiant jewels.

- **Pranic Flow:** Deeply inhale and exhale, directing the energy flow in a circuit – descending down one side of your body and ascending on the opposite side, doing this three times.

4. Front and Back Body Circulation:

- **Energy Cascade:** Visualize the energy flowing from the crown to the feet along the front as you exhale, and rising along the back as you inhale, repeating this cycle three times.

5. Central Channel Activation:

- **Core Energy Fountain:** Envision energy gathering at your feet, then rising through the central axis of your body, akin to a Kundalini awakening. As it reaches the crown, imagine it cascading down like a fountain of light, enveloping you in a protective and revitalizing energy field.

- **Repetition:** Perform this willpower several times until you feel an equilibrium of energy throughout your being.

This meditation, deeply rooted in Indian spiritual practices, is a powerful tool for activating the body's pranic energy and harmonizing the chakras. It encourages the free flow of energy, leading to a state of holistic well-being, energized tranquility, and heightened awareness.

Crafting Your Inner Haven: An Indian-Inspired Willpower for Serenity and Strength

This willpower technique, deeply rooted in Indian meditative practices, is designed to create an inner sanctuary – a personal haven of peace, which you can visit at any time to rejuvenate and empower yourself.

1. Preparation:

- **Comfort:** Find a tranquil spot, sit in a comfortable Padmasana (lotus position) or any relaxed posture. Close your eyes, allowing the rhythms of your breathing to guide you into relaxation.
- **Initial Relaxation:** Channel your focus inward, letting go of external distractions, embodying a sense of calm.

2. Crafting Your Haven:

- **Visualizing a Natural Setting:** Imagine a serene natural environment that resonates with you. It could be a lush forest akin to the Western Ghats, a tranquil beach reminiscent of the Konkan coast, or the serene Himalayan foothills. Let this place be your canvas.
- **Engage Your Senses:** Immerse in the vivid details of this place - the sounds, the colors, the scents. Each sensory detail brings you deeper into the tranquility of your haven.

3. Personalizing Your Space:

- **Creating Comfort:** In this natural abode, envision creating a space that reflects your essence. Perhaps a simple cottage with Vastu Shastra elements, a serene meditation corner, or a garden of vibrant Indian flora.
- **Protective Aura:** Envision the entire area enveloped in a golden light, symbolizing protection and safety, ensuring this sanctuary remains untouched and pure.

4. Regular Visits:

- **Accessible Retreat:** Recognize this sanctuary as your personal retreat. You can retreat here whenever you seek peace or need to reconnect with your inner strength.
- **Adaptation and Growth:** Allow this space to evolve with you. Your haven might change, reflecting your growth and current needs. Embrace these changes, knowing your haven is a reflection of your inner self.

5. Embracing Peace and Power:

- **Meditative Sojourns:** Regularly visiting your sanctuary during meditation enhances its healing and empowering qualities. Each visit strengthens your connection to this inner world of tranquility and insight.

By incorporating elements of Indian spirituality and environmental richness, this willpower practice serves not just as a method for relaxation but also as a tool for personal empowerment, reflecting the rich tapestry of Indian culture and spiritual wisdom.

Communing with Your Inner Sage: An Indian-Inspired Guided Meditation

This meditation draws from the rich Indian tradition of inner reflection and guidance. It's designed to connect you with your inner sage or guide, a source of wisdom deeply rooted in your subconscious, akin to the concept of the 'Guru' within.

1. Preparation:

- **Relaxation:** Find a serene place, ideally where you won't be disturbed. Sit comfortably, perhaps in Sukhasana (easy pose), and gently close your eyes. Take deep breaths, focusing on releasing tension with each exhale.

2. Journey to Your Inner Sanctuary:

- **Willpower:** Imagine yourself in a serene, sacred space. This could be a depiction of a tranquil ashram, a Himalayan cave, or a peaceful grove by the Ganges. Spend a few moments here, letting the peace of this place permeate your being.

- **Pathway to Wisdom:** Visualize a path leading deeper into your sanctuary. Notice its details – perhaps it's lined with marigolds or leads past a gently flowing stream.

3. Meeting Your Inner Guide:

- **Approaching the Guide:** As you walk along the path, visualize a figure approaching you, radiating calm and wisdom. Observe their features as they become clearer - maybe they resemble a sage, a deity from Indian mythology, or a revered Guru.

- **First Interaction:** Greet this figure with respect, as you would a wise mentor. Ask for their name, accepting the first name that comes to your mind.

4. Receiving Wisdom:

- **Guided Exploration:** Allow your guide to show you around your sanctuary. Be open to new insights or areas of your sanctuary they may reveal.

- **Seeking Advice:** Engage in a conversation. You may ask questions about your life, seek guidance, or simply listen to what they have to share. Remember, the dialogue may not always be verbal; it can manifest as feelings or images.

5. Conclusion:

- **Gratitude and Farewell:** Once you feel the interaction is complete, express your gratitude to your guide. Ask them to join you again in future meditations.

- **Return to Awareness:** Slowly bring your consciousness back to your physical surroundings. Open your eyes when ready, carrying any wisdom or peace back with you.

By integrating aspects of Indian spiritual and cultural heritage, this meditation not only helps you find guidance but also connects you with the profound wisdom that resides within, much like the teachings of the Upanishads and the Bhagavad Gita emphasize the importance of inner knowledge and self-realization.

Encountering Your Inner Mentor: An Indian-Inspired Meditative Practice

In this Indian-inspired meditative journey, you'll discover your Inner Mentor, a spiritual guide embodying wisdom and guidance. Drawing from India's rich tapestry of spiritual teachings, this practice offers a path to inner clarity and serenity.

1. Setting the Stage:

- **Relaxation:** Choose a peaceful spot, perhaps decorated with elements like incense or a Diya (lamp) to create a serene atmosphere. Sit comfortably, perhaps in the Lotus position, and gently close your eyes. Breathe deeply, releasing tension with each exhale.

2. Journey to the Inner Realm:

- **Visualizing the Sacred Space:** Imagine a tranquil place, like a serene Himalayan cave or a verdant Rishikesh riverside. Absorb the tranquility and peace around you.

- **Path of Enlightenment:** Visualize a pathway leading deeper into this sacred space. Observe its nuances – perhaps adorned with Rudraksha beads or lined with sacred texts.

3. Meeting Your Inner Mentor:

- **Approaching the Mentor:** As you traverse the path, envisage a figure radiating wisdom and serenity approaching you. Notice their attire – maybe reflecting a sage, a deity, or a revered Guru.

- **Engagement and Dialogue:** Greet this figure with reverence. Ask their name, accepting the first name that comes to mind. Engage in dialogue, seeking insights or guidance, responding to feelings or visions.

4. Embracing the Wisdom:

- **Guidance:** Let your mentor guide you through your inner realm. Be open to any wisdom or areas revealed.

- **Inquiry:** Seek answers or guidance on matters close to your heart. Be receptive to the mentor's method of communication.

5. Concluding the Experience:

- **Gratitude and Departure:** After your interaction, express gratitude to your mentor. Request their presence in future meditations.

- **Returning to Consciousness:** Gradually bring your awareness back to your surroundings. Open your eyes, carrying the serenity and wisdom back into your world.

This meditation integrates elements of Indian spirituality, such as the concept of the 'Antar Guru' (inner teacher) and the teachings of the Upanishads on self-knowledge. It's designed to guide you to deep introspection and realization, connecting with the profound wisdom that resides within.

Manifesting with the Heart's Hue: An Indian-Inspired Willpower Practice

This willpower technique, infused with Indian spiritual elements, focuses on manifesting your desires using the color pink, associated with Anahata (the heart chakra) in Indian tradition, symbolizing love, warmth, and emotional well-being.

1. Preparation:

- **Finding Serenity:** Choose a quiet, peaceful environment. You might want to sit on a traditional Indian Baithak or a simple mat.

- **Relaxation:** Close your eyes and take deep, slow breaths. Imagine the soothing sound of temple bells or the gentle rustle of leaves in the wind, allowing your body and mind to relax.

2. Envisioning Your Desire:

- **Manifesting Vision:** Think of a goal or wish you deeply desire. Visualize it vividly, like watching a scene from a Bollywood movie, full of color and life.

- **Embracing the Pink Glow:** Envision your goal encased in a radiant pink bubble. This hue, reminiscent of the soft petals of the Indian lotus, represents the purity and compassion of the heart.

3. Releasing to the Universe:

- **Letting Go:** Gently release the pink bubble, allowing it to drift upwards, like a lantern in the sky during Diwali, symbolizing liberation and ascent.

- **Emotional Release:** As the bubble floats away, feel a sense of detachment, signifying your trust in the universe (Brahman), the ultimate source of all creation.

4. Affirmation and Closure:

- **Affirmative Faith:** Silently affirm to yourself in Sanskrit or your preferred language, "May my desires manifest in harmony with the universe."

- **Concluding the Meditation:** Slowly bring your awareness back to the present, opening your eyes with gratitude and a sense of peace.

This practice aligns with the principles of Dharma and Karma in Indian philosophy, emphasizing desire in alignment with the cosmic law and the importance of letting go, entrusting the universe to manifest in divine timing. It's an exercise in balancing personal aspirations with universal harmony.

Invigorating Wholeness: An Indian-Inspired Guide to Healing Meditation

This meditation technique, rooted in Indian wellness traditions, aims to promote healing and understanding of physical ailments through a blend of relaxation, willpower, and introspection.

1. Preparatory Relaxation:

- **Position and Breathing:** Sit comfortably or lie down, adopting a relaxed posture. Imagine the serene environment of a Himalayan ashram. Breathe deeply, letting each breath guide you to a state of calm.

- **Body Awareness:** Starting at your toes, gently focus on each part of your body. Visualize the tension melting away, like the dissolving of mist at dawn.

2. Engaging with Energy Centers:

- **Visualizing Healing Energy:** Picture a soothing golden light enveloping your body, reminiscent of the warm glow of the morning sun over the Ganges. Feel its healing essence.

- **Addressing Specific Areas:** If there is any area of your body that needs attention, imagine directing a concentrated beam of this light to it.

3. Communicating with the Self:

- **Intuitive Inquiry:** Gently ask the area of discomfort if it holds any message or insight for you. Be open to receiving words, images, or sensations as responses.

- **Interpreting Responses:** If you receive an answer, acknowledge and ponder its significance. If not, remain patient; insights can surface unexpectedly later.

4. Willpower for Healing:

- **Empowering Healing:** Envision the specific problem or pain dissipating, being replaced by vibrant health. You may invoke the presence of a healing figure from Indian mythology or spirituality to aid in this willpower.

- **Holistic Well-being:** Picture yourself in various life scenarios, radiating health and vitality. Embrace images of engaging in activities that bring you joy and wellness.

5. Cultivating Self-care:

- **Commitment to Health:** Visualize yourself practicing daily routines that contribute to your well-being, inspired by Ayurvedic principles or Yoga practices.

- **Closing the Meditation:** Gradually bring your awareness back to your surroundings, carrying with you a sense of renewed health and a commitment to nurturing your well-being.

This meditation blends the ancient wisdom of Indian spiritual practices with modern willpower techniques, fostering a holistic approach to health that encompasses physical, emotional, and spiritual dimensions.

Empowerments for Holistic Well-being: An Indian-Inspired Self-Care Mantra

This series of empowerments, deeply rooted in the Indian philosophy of holistic health, emphasizes the unity of mind, body, spirit, and emotions. It encourages a respectful and nurturing relationship with the self, drawing upon traditional Indian wisdom and contemporary wellness practices.

1. Embracing Wholeness:

- **Spiritual Connection:** "I am nurturing my spirit with the wisdom of the Vedas and Upanishads."
- **Mental Clarity:** "In the stillness of meditation, my mind finds clarity and peace."
- **Emotional Balance:** "I embrace my emotions with the compassion of Buddha, learning from their depths."
- **Physical Health:** "I honor the temple of my body, nourishing it with Ayurvedic principles."

2. Body Reverence:

- **Respectful Attunement:** "I listen to the sacred whispers of my body, understanding its needs and messages."
- **Self-Care Commitment:** "I pledge to care for myself with the gentle touch of a loving caregiver."
- **Complete Acceptance:** "I embrace my physical form with the unconditional love of the divine."

3. Symbiotic Relationship:

- **Body Gratitude:** "I am thankful for the strength and vitality of my body, which supports me in all my endeavors."
- **Mutual Care:** "As I treat my body with kindness, it responds with robust health and energy."

4. Harmonious Existence:

- **Inner and Outer Balance:** "My being is in harmonious alignment with the rhythms of nature and the cosmos."

- **Thankfulness for Well-being:** "With every breath, I express gratitude for increasing health, beauty, and vitality."

- **Natural Wellness:** "Feeling good is my inherent right, and I embrace it wholeheartedly."

5. Willpower of Health:

- **Perfect Health Imagery:** "In moments of quietude, I visualize myself radiating health, encircled by a halo of healing golden light."

These empowerments blend the time-honored wisdom of Indian spirituality and philosophy with modern understandings of health and well-being, creating a powerful tool for anyone seeking to nurture their holistic health. They are designed to be recited daily, serving as reminders of the interconnected nature of our existence and the importance of honoring every aspect of our being.

Guidance for Energetic Healing from an Indian Cultural Perspective

This narrative presents a spiritual and meditative approach to healing others, deeply influenced by Indian cultural and spiritual practices, and incorporating elements of modern holistic health philosophies.

1. Preparing for the Healing Journey:

- **Inner Harmony:** Begin by attaining a state of deep tranquility. Engage in Pranayama (breath control) or a brief session of Yoga Nidra to cultivate inner peace.

- **Channeling Universal Energy:** Visualize yourself as a mere conduit for the cosmic energy. This life force, akin to Prana, flows through you but is not of you.

2. Visualizing the Healing Process:

- **Creating a Mental Image:** Gently bring the image of the person you wish to heal into your mind's eye. If you know their favorite deity or spiritual symbol, imagine this figure bestowing blessings upon them.

- **Specific Healing Intentions:** If guided to address particular ailments, visualize those body parts rejuvenating and glowing with health, as if the divine nectar, Amrit, is being poured onto them.

3. Infusing the Person with Positive Energy:

- **Golden Light Willpower:** Envelop the individual in a radiant golden aura. This light, reminiscent of the divine aura seen in traditional Indian art, symbolizes perfect health and vitality.

- **Affirmative Mental Dialogue:** Convey to the person, through the power of thought, that they are nurtured by the universal spirit. Use empowerments inspired by Upanishads to reinforce their healing.

4. Concluding the Healing Session:

- **Visualizing Complete Wellness:** As you draw the session to a close, hold the image of the person in robust health. Imagine them participating in activities they love, radiating joy and vitality.

- **Releasing to the Universe:** Gently release the image of the person, entrusting their wellbeing to the higher cosmic forces. Chant a mantra or a Shanti path (peace hymn) to conclude.

5. Post-Healing Practice:

- **Continued Positive Willpower:** In your daily meditations, maintain the vision of the individual's perfect health. Refrain from focusing on the illness; instead, visualize their life filled with happiness and health.

- **Energetic Balance:** If at any point you feel drained, step back and reaffirm your role as a channel rather than a source. Practice grounding exercises, like visualizing roots extending from your feet deep into Mother Earth, to reestablish your energetic balance.

In this approach, the healer remains a humble facilitator, channeling the boundless universal energy for the welfare of others, while also ensuring their own spiritual and energetic health. This method is deeply respectful of both the healer's and the recipient's spiritual journey.

Group Healing: An Indian Spiritual Perspective

This narrative outlines a group healing session, deeply rooted in Indian spiritual practices, and influenced by ancient wisdom from the Vedas and Upanishads. It incorporates elements of traditional Indian healing rituals, ensuring a holistic and spiritually enriching experience for all participants.

1. Setting the Sacred Space:

- **Formation of Healing Circle:** Gather participants around the person in need of healing, either seated or lying down at the center. Arrange seating in a circular pattern to symbolize the cycle of life and energy.

- **Sanctifying the Environment:** Initiate the session with a short prayer or mantra from the Upanishads to invoke divine presence and create a sacred healing atmosphere.

2. Channeling Collective Energy:

- **Guided Willpower:** Guide participants to close their eyes and visualize a stream of healing energy emanating from their hearts, converging towards the individual at the center.

- **Incorporating Ancient Wisdom:** Use teachings from the Vedas to deepen understanding of the healing process. For instance, discuss the concept of Prana (life force) and its role in healing.

3. The Healing Process:

- **Energy Transmission:** Encourage participants to extend their hands towards the person, imagining Pranic energy flowing through their palms, engulfing the individual in a healing aura.

- **Chanting for Vibrational Healing:** Introduce the chanting of "Om," explaining its significance as the primal sound of the universe, as mentioned in the Upanishads. This creates a powerful healing vibration.

4. For Absent Individuals:

- **Distance Healing:** If the person to be healed is not physically present, inform participants of their name and location. Emphasize the Vedic teaching that energy is not confined by physical boundaries and can travel across distances.

- **Visualizing Distant Healing:** Have participants focus their energy towards the absent individual, visualizing them enveloped in a radiant, healing light.

5. Concluding the Session:

- **Gratitude and Blessings:** End the session with a thanksgiving prayer or a peaceful chant from the Vedas, expressing gratitude to the divine for facilitating the healing.
- **Sharing Insights:** Allow time for participants to share their experiences and insights, fostering a sense of community and collective spiritual growth.

Through this approach, the group healing session becomes a deeply spiritual experience, blending traditional Indian healing practices with contemporary group dynamics, and enhancing the collective consciousness towards healing and well-being.

Healing Through Color Willpower: A Meditative Approach for Alleviating Pain

In this narrative, we explore an Indian-inspired meditation technique for pain relief, focusing on the concept of color willpower, deeply influenced by ancient Indian wisdom and practices.

1. Preparation and Relaxation:

- **Initiating Relaxation:** Guide the individual to lie down comfortably, ensuring a tranquil environment, possibly with soft Indian instrumental music in the background to enhance relaxation.
- **Deep Breathing Exercise:** Encourage deep, slow breaths, suggesting they mentally count from ten to one, aligning with the Indian practice of Pranayama for deeper relaxation.

2. Willpower of Healing Colors:

- **Color Sphere Creation:** Instruct the individual to imagine a bright color (the first that comes to mind), visualizing it as a sphere of light, about six inches in diameter. This is based on the Indian belief in colors as powerful healing tools.

- **Expansion and Contraction of Color Sphere:** Guide them to gradually expand this sphere until it encompasses their entire mental vision, then slowly contract it back to its original size, and eventually to a point where it disappears. This process symbolizes the expansion and contraction of the universe, a concept from the Upanishads.

3. Associating Pain with Color:

- **Color as a Symbol of Pain:** Next, instruct them to visualize the color as representing their pain. This aligns with Ayurvedic teachings where colors are associated with specific bodily elements and sensations.

- **Manipulating the Pain Symbol:** Have them repeat the process of expanding and shrinking the colored sphere, this time with the intention that the sphere symbolizes their pain.

4. Dissolving the Pain:

- **Willpower of Pain Reduction:** As they reduce the size of the sphere, encourage them to feel their pain diminishing simultaneously. The shrinking sphere acts as a metaphor for their pain lessening and eventually disappearing.

5. Completing the Meditation:

- **Final Relaxation and Awareness:** After the pain symbol has vanished, guide them to stay in a relaxed state, breathing deeply. Encourage them to become aware of their body, acknowledging any relief or changes in pain perception.

- **Gratitude and Closing:** Conclude the session with a moment of gratitude, possibly incorporating a short verse from the Upanishads to honor the healing process and the universal energies.

This technique combines traditional Indian practices with modern meditative exercises, offering a holistic and culturally enriched approach to managing pain through meditation and the power of willpower.

Invoking Inner Qualities: An Indian-Inspired Meditative Approach

This narrative outlines a meditative practice deeply rooted in the Indian tradition of invoking inner qualities and energies, drawing inspiration from the Vedic and Upanishadic wisdom.

1. Preparing for Meditation:

- **Initial Relaxation:** Begin by finding a peaceful space, adopting a comfortable posture, and focusing on deep, rhythmic breathing to attain a state of relaxation. This mirrors the Indian practice of Pranayama for calming the mind.

- **Energy Activation:** Use techniques like grounding or opening energy centers, reminiscent of the Chakra system in Indian traditions, to enhance energy flow.

2. Invoking the Desired Quality:

- **Articulating the Invocation:** Silently yet assertively, declare the intention to summon a specific quality, such as love, wisdom, or serenity. This aligns with the Indian concept of Sankalpa (intention-setting).

- **Experiencing the Energy:** Immerse in the sensation of the invoked energy, feeling it fill and radiate from within, akin to the concept of Prana or life force in Indian philosophy.

3. Directing the Energy:

- **Willpower and Affirmation:** Channel the energy towards a particular goal or vision, using empowerments and willpower techniques, reflecting the Indian tradition of using positive empowerments (Mantras).

4. Invoking Inspirational Figures:

- **Summoning Universal Qualities:** Invoke the spirit or essence of revered figures such as Buddha, Christ, or Mary, symbolizing universal qualities. This practice echoes the Indian tradition of evoking deities or gurus for their symbolic virtues.

- **Selective Invocation:** Focus on the positive aspects and virtues of the chosen figure, disregarding any personal flaws, to harness their highest qualities.

5. Applying to Personal Development:

- **Skill and Talent Enhancement:** For personal growth in areas like music or art, invoke the spirit of a great master in the field, envisioning their support and channeling their creative genius.

- **Selective Quality Absorption:** Emulate only the positive attributes of these figures, leaving aside any personal limitations they might have had.

This meditative practice effectively combines the ancient Indian wisdom of inner energy harnessing and the power of invocation to cultivate desired qualities, illustrating a holistic approach to personal development and spiritual well-being.

Empowering Empowerments: Manifesting Positivity and Transformation

Harnessing the wisdom of the Vedas and Upanishads, and blending it with contemporary insights and practicality, let's explore the various profound ways to use empowerments effectively for personal growth, positivity, and goal achievement within the Indian context.

1. Empowerments in Meditation:

- **Silent Meditation Empowerments:** During your meditation or deep relaxation sessions, silently recite empowerments. This practice syncs with ancient Indian techniques of self-contemplation and introspection, akin to Dhyana and Pratyahara.

- **Morning and Evening Empowerments:** Empowerments can be particularly potent when recited before sunrise or right before sleep, aligning with the traditional Indian practice of Surya Namaskar (Salutation to the Sun) and bedtime reflections.

2. Spoken Empowerments:

- **Daily Verbal Repetition:** Regularly repeat empowerments aloud or silently throughout the day. Incorporate them into your daily routine, such as during chores or while driving. This mirrors the idea of Japa (chanting) in Indian spirituality.

- **Mirror Empowerments:** Stand before a mirror, look into your own eyes, and confidently recite empowerments. This practice nurtures self-esteem and self-love, aligning with the essence of Atman (the inner self) and self-acceptance in Indian philosophy.

- **Recording and Playback:** Use modern technology to record your empowerments on a device and play them during various activities. Address yourself in the first, second, and third person, resembling the idea of self-reflective dialogue in Upanishadic teachings.

3. Written Empowerments:

- **Repetitive Writing:** Repetitively write a chosen affirmation, reflecting upon the words with each repetition. Gradually refine and enhance the affirmation, mirroring the concept of 'Abhyasa' (persistent practice) in yoga philosophy.

- **Visual Reminders:** Write or type empowerments and place them strategically around your living and working spaces as visual reminders. This practice resembles the ancient tradition of sacred symbols and yantras in Indian culture.

By weaving these empowerments into your daily life, you integrate ancient and contemporary wisdom, fostering personal transformation, self-love, and positive manifestation. Just as a yogi hones their asanas or a scholar studies the scriptures, the art of affirmation can become an integral part of your spiritual journey, nurturing your mind, body, and soul.

Empowering Empowerments in Relationships: Building Bonds of Positivity

In the rich tapestry of human connections, empowerments can be a potent thread that weaves positivity, love, and support. Let's delve into how empowerments can strengthen relationships, drawing inspiration from Indian philosophy and modern wisdom.

1. Empowerments with a Partner:

- **Partnered Empowerments:** Sit facing your friend or loved one, gazing into each other's eyes. Take turns affirming positive qualities about each other.
  - Example:
    - Leela: "Priya, your beauty, love, and creativity shine brightly."
    - Umesha: "Yes, I embrace my beauty, love, and creativity."
- Repeat this exchange genuinely and repeatedly, allowing the empowerments to sink in. Switch roles so that both individuals receive empowerments.

2. Informal Empowerments among Friends:

- **Friendly Empowerments:** Encourage your friends to affirm positive qualities in you informally. For instance, if you aim to enhance your communication skills, ask a friend to affirm your progress frequently.
  - Example: Priya: "You're certainly expressing yourself more clearly these days, Priya!"
- Turn it into a playful game where you reciprocate with empowerments for your friends. Embrace the power of supportive feedback from friends, aligning with the Indian tradition of community and mutual upliftment.

3. Integrating Empowerments in Conversations:

- **Conversational Empowerments:** Infuse your daily conversations with positive statements about people and situations. Consciously choose words that radiate positivity.

- This practice transforms the tone of your interactions and aligns with the principle of 'Satyam Vada' (Speak the truth) from ancient Indian scriptures, emphasizing the importance of truthful and positive speech.

A word of wisdom: Employ empowerments authentically, avoiding contradiction with your true emotions. In moments of distress or negativity, refrain from using empowerments, allowing yourself to acknowledge and address your feelings. Instead, apply empowerments constructively from a place of positivity to reshape your subconscious thought patterns and beliefs.

By integrating empowerments into your relationships, you foster an environment of mutual empowerment, nurturing bonds that are deeply rooted in positivity, understanding, and growth. Just as the lotus blooms amidst the mud, your relationships can flourish with the power of empowerments.

Harmonious Melodies: Singing and Chanting for Transformation

In the vibrant tapestry of life, the power of music and empowerments can be harnessed to navigate the journey within. Let's explore how the fusion of music and self-empowerments, deeply rooted in Indian wisdom, can lead to personal growth and transformation.

1. Singing and Chanting:

- **Soulful Songs:** Embrace songs that resonate with your innermost feelings and aspirations. These melodies can serve as a vehicle for self-expression and affirmation.

- Example: Immerse yourself in the verses of the timeless "Bhagavad Gita," where Lord Krishna imparts wisdom to Arjuna on the battlefield, offering guidance and clarity during life's struggles. Sing or listen to these verses to draw strength and wisdom.

- **Compose Your Chants:** Craft your own chants and songs using empowerments that align with your goals and desires. These personalized chants become a reflection of your inner intentions.

  - Example: Create a chant that encapsulates your journey towards self-acceptance:

- "I accept myself wholly and unconditionally, In this moment, I am complete and free. All emotions within me, I embrace with glee, For they are parts of my unique tapestry."

2. Embracing Self-Acceptance:

- **Accepting Oneself:** Embrace the essence of self-acceptance through empowerments. Internalize the belief that you are beautiful and lovable, regardless of your emotional state.

  - Example: Reflect on the Upanishadic principle, "Aham Brahmasmi" (I am the divine). Affirm:

- "I accept myself as a divine creation, pure and whole. My feelings, diverse and profound, define my soul. None are negative; they complete me as a whole, I now allow and express them, for that is my goal."

- **Inviting Joy:** Allow yourself to experience joy and pleasure without reservations. Cultivate an environment that encourages happiness and self-love.

- o Example: Draw inspiration from the joyful tales of Lord Krishna, who celebrated life with music and dance. Affirm:
- "I revel in the moments that bring me delight, Joy flows freely, and my heart feels light. Like Krishna's dance on a moonlit night, I embrace life's rhythms, oh, what a sight!"

3. Nurturing Relationships:

- **Mirror of Relationships:** Recognize that relationships reflect your inner self. Empowerments can guide you in learning and growing through these connections.
  - o Example: Referencing the Mahabharata, where the Pandavas' bond represents unity and strength, affirm:
    - "My relationships mirror my soul's true quest, They teach me lessons, and I am blessed. With strength, vulnerability, love as my crest, I deserve love and joy, for I am divinely dressed."
- **Divine Attraction:** Cultivate empowerments that resonate with your intention to attract fulfilling relationships.
  - o Example: Channel the divine love stories of Radha and Krishna for inspiration:
    - "Radiating love from the depths of my heart, I'm ready for love's magical, transformative art. Just as Radha's devotion set her apart, My perfect mate, divinely, we'll chart."

4. Unleashing Creativity:

- **Creative Channel:** Affirm your creative potential as an open channel for innovative ideas and inspiration.

- Example: Recall the genius of ancient scholars like Aryabhata. Affirm:

- "I am a conduit for creativity's divine stream, Ideas and inspiration, like a vivid dream. As Aryabhata's wisdom did gleam, I create my destiny, as it may seem."

5. Divine Guidance:

- **Guided by the Divine:** Embrace empowerments that align with the guidance of a higher power and your inner wisdom.
  - Example: Reflect on the spiritual guidance of the Bhagavad Gita. Affirm:

- "In the vast expanse of the divine's embrace, Guided by the Gita, I find my place. With inner wisdom as my saving grace, I journey with purpose, at a steady pace."

6. Miraculous Transformation:

- **The Power of Light:** Believe in the transformative power of divine light and love to bring miracles into your life.
  - Example: Meditate on the radiance of the enlightened ones. Affirm:

- "Within me, the light sparks a miraculous dance, Body, mind, and life, in its radiant trance. Like enlightened sages in timeless expanse, Miracles manifest, in every circumstance."

Let the symphony of empowerments and melodies guide you on a transformative journey, where the ancient wisdom of India and contemporary insights merge to nurture your inner growth and self-realization. Like the river of life, your empowerments flow, shaping your reality and leading you towards a more harmonious and empowered existence.

Part 4
Advanced Methods: Mastering Manifestation Techniques

Discovering the Divine Essence Within: A Path to Right Relations

In the pursuit of harmonious relationships and a deeper understanding of the world, let us embark on a journey inspired by the timeless wisdom of India, where we seek the divine within all beings and trust in the providence of the universe.

The Divine Essence Within:

- **Sacred Vision:** To cultivate right relations, we must first adopt a sacred vision. The Upanishads guide us, saying, "Tat Tvam Asi" (Thou art That). This teaching reminds us that the divine essence resides in every being, making each soul a spark of the divine cosmic consciousness.

- **The River of Humanity:** Picture a vast river representing humanity. Just as the Ganga flows through India, symbolizing purity, so does the divine essence flow through all souls. We must navigate this river with reverence for the divine presence within every individual.

Leaving the Rest to God:

- **The Law of Karma:** In our quest for right relations, we encounter the law of karma. The Bhagavad Gita advises, "You have the right to perform your prescribed duties, but you are not entitled to the fruits of your actions." By focusing on our actions, rather than outcomes, we align with divine order.

- **Trust in Providence:** The Bhagavad Gita also teaches us to surrender to the divine will, saying, "Let thy will be done." Just as Lord Rama trusted in the divine guidance of Lord Hanuman, we too can surrender our worries to the divine and trust in the unfolding of events.

Stories of Divine Encounters:

- **The Meeting of Souls:** Recall the tale of Lord Krishna and Sudama, childhood friends separated by circumstances. When Sudama visited Lord Krishna in Dwarka, he was humbly received. Lord Krishna recognized the divine in Sudama and showered him with blessings, emphasizing the importance of true friendship and recognizing the divine in each other.

- **The Compassion of the Buddha:** In another story, inspired by the life of Lord Buddha, we learn of his encounter with Angulimala, a notorious bandit. Instead of condemning Angulimala for his past deeds, Lord Buddha saw the divine potential within him. Through compassion and wisdom, he transformed Angulimala into a noble disciple.

Embracing Modern Insights:

- **Psychology of Perception:** Modern psychology reminds us of the power of perception. When we view others with a positive mindset, we often elicit positive responses in return. Embracing this insight, we consciously choose to perceive the divine essence in everyone.

- **Empathy and Compassion:** Scientific studies emphasize the benefits of empathy and compassion in building strong relationships. By acknowledging the divine within, we naturally foster empathy and compassion, enriching our interactions.

The Path to Right Relations: As we navigate the labyrinth of human connections, let us remember the words of J. Allen Boone, "Look only for the divine in people and things, and leave all the rest to God." In this journey, we honor the teachings of the Vedas and Upanishads, drawing inspiration from ancient wisdom while applying contemporary insights. By recognizing the divine essence within ourselves and others, we embark on a path of harmony, compassion, and spiritual growth, nurturing right relations that reflect the divine tapestry of existence.

The Pioneering Thinking Journal: A Canvas of Manifestation

In our pursuit of self-realization and the actualization of our deepest desires, let us embark on a journey through the pages of a Pioneering Thinking Journal inspired by the wisdom of India. Within this journal, we shall explore various exercises and practices designed to harness the power of our thoughts and intentions, all while integrating the essence of Indian philosophy.

Nurturing Your Inner World:

- **Empowerments - Mantras for the Soul:** Begin your journal with a section dedicated to your favorite empowerments, reminiscent of the sacred mantras found in Indian traditions. Write them down with ornate borders and designs, allowing the act of writing to transform into a meditation, instilling each word with profound meaning.

- **The Outpouring of Energy:** Create a list of ways in which you can outflow your energy into the world, akin to the concept of 'seva' or selfless service in Hinduism. Include acts of kindness, generosity, and contributions to your community and loved ones. As you continually add to this list, you magnify your positive impact on the world.

- **The Tapestry of Success:** Document your personal successes and achievements in all facets of life, acknowledging that success extends beyond the material realm. Celebrate your victories, both big and small, and let this list serve as a testament to your abilities and potential.

- **The Gratitude Bouquet:** Craft a bouquet of appreciation, listing all the things you are thankful for and deeply appreciate in your life. Much like the concept of 'prasad' in Hinduism, this practice opens your heart to the abundance that surrounds you.

- **The Portrait of Self-Love:** Devote a section to listing all the qualities you love about yourself, emphasizing that self-love is not an ego trip but a means to radiate love and positivity into the world.

- **The Acts of Self-Care:** Create a catalog of ways to nurture and pamper yourself, reflecting the practice of 'self-care' found in Ayurveda. Include simple daily indulgences that promote your well-being, fostering a clear and positive mindset for creating your desired life.

- **Healing and Support:** Maintain a list of individuals in need of healing and support, embodying the spirit of 'metta' or loving-kindness meditation. Alongside their names, write special empowerments or prayers for their well-being, knowing that your energy can uplift and heal.

- **Dreams and Creative Insights:** Dedicate a space to jot down your dreams, aspirations, and creative ideas. Much like the concept of 'darshan' where seekers receive divine insight, consider every idea a potential seed for manifestation.

Balancing the Inner and Outer Realms: While it may seem challenging to allocate time for your journal amidst a busy life, remember that nurturing your inner world through these practices yields remarkable results on the external plane. A few minutes each day or a dedicated hour every week can foster transformative growth that far exceeds the invested time.

Embracing Contemporary Tools: In the age of technology, consider incorporating the latest digital tools and apps that aid in Pioneering Thinking and self-improvement, merging ancient wisdom with modern convenience.

As you traverse the sacred pages of your Pioneering Thinking Journal, may you experience the profound transformation that occurs when thoughts align with intentions. This sacred space becomes a canvas where the divine essence within you meets the boundless potential of the universe, painting the masterpiece of your life.

Overcoming Inner Obstacles: A Journey of Self-Discovery

In our pursuit of Pioneering Thinking and self-realization, we often encounter inner blocks that hinder our progress towards our highest potential. These "blocks" are the dams in the river of our consciousness, where energy stagnates and impedes the free flow of our aspirations. In the profound tapestry of Indian wisdom, let us explore how to recognize, accept, and release these blocks, drawing inspiration from the Vedas and Upanishads.

The Nature of Blocks: Unveiling the Constriction Blocks in our consciousness typically stem from repressed emotions like fear, sadness, guilt, self-criticism, and resentment. These emotions cause us to contract spiritually, mentally, emotionally, and even physically. In the ancient scriptures, it is said that the mind is like a river, and when it encounters obstacles (blocks), it loses its flow and clarity.

To address these blocks effectively, we must embark on a two-fold journey:

1. Acceptance and Release:

- Mentally and emotionally embrace the feelings locked within the block, allowing them to flow freely. This acceptance manifests as relaxation and release, echoing the concept of 'santosha' or contentment in yoga philosophy.

2. Clear Observation and Understanding:

- Through keen observation, seek to understand the root of the problem, often concealed by limiting attitudes or beliefs. In the Upanishads, it is taught that self-realization arises from deep introspection and discernment.

The Alchemical Process: Transforming Beliefs In the pursuit of dissolving these blocks, we must simultaneously practice self-compassion and discernment. Here, we shall unveil some common core beliefs that may resonate with your inner journey:

1. **I'm not okay; there's something wrong with me.** In the wisdom of the Vedas, we find the concept of 'Atman,' the inner self, which is inherently pure and divine. Recognize your innate worthiness.

2. **I've done bad things and deserve suffering.** The path of karma in Hinduism emphasizes the potential for

redemption and growth. Accept your past, learn, and evolve.

3. **People are inherently bad.** Reflect on the teachings of Lord Krishna in the Bhagavad Gita, where he explains the interplay of virtues and vices within us. People are multifaceted, and the choice to nurture goodness lies within.

4. **The world is an unsafe place.** Invoke the protection of deities like Goddess Durga, symbolizing fearlessness and divine safeguarding. Trust in the balance of the universe.

5. **There's not enough to go around.** Explore the philosophy of 'aparigraha' (non-possessiveness) from Jainism, emphasizing contentment and detachment from material desires.

6. **Life is suffering.** Embrace the teachings of Buddha on the path to Nirvana, where the cessation of suffering is the ultimate goal. Seek inner peace and joy.

7. **Love and power are dangerous.** Recall the wise words of Swami Vivekananda, advocating for the responsible use of power and the transformative power of love.

8. **Money is corrupt.** In the spirit of 'Dhana' (prosperity) from the Rigveda, perceive wealth as a tool for good, charity, and spiritual growth.

9. **The world is worsening.** The Bhagavad Gita teaches the cyclical nature of existence. Trust in the grand cosmic design.

10. **I lack control.** Harness the 'tapas' (discipline) of self-control, as emphasized in the Upanishads, to shape your destiny.

The Power to Transform: While these beliefs may appear daunting collectively, they are but beliefs, not objective truths. As you read through them, recognize that every one of us has, to varying degrees, embraced these viewpoints due to societal conditioning. Yet, the beauty lies in our capacity to alter these beliefs and, consequently, our reality.

Harness the power within you to shift your beliefs about life, humanity, and reality. In doing so, you embark on a transformative journey that not only impacts your life but also contributes to the evolving consciousness of the world. The Vedas and Upanishads, along with modern wisdom, offer tools for this profound inner alchemy. This journal provides you with a sacred space to embark on this transformative odyssey.

Unlocking Inner Barriers: A Journey to Self-Realization

In our quest for personal growth and self-realization, we often encounter inner obstacles that hinder our progress. These barriers, though intangible, hold immense power over our ability to manifest our desires. In this transformative journey, we will explore clearing exercises inspired by Indian wisdom, modern psychology, and the latest insights in self-improvement.

Exercise 1: Unmasking Limiting Beliefs

Begin by taking a piece of paper and inscribing at the top, "The reason I can't have what I want is..." Allow your thoughts to flow freely and without judgment as you complete this sentence. List about twenty or thirty thoughts that surface, no matter how trivial they may seem. Here's a sample to start:

"The reason I can't have what I want is...

- I'm too lazy.
- I don't have enough money.

- It doesn't exist.
- I've tried before and it never worked.
- Mother said I couldn't.
- I don't want to.
- It's too hard.
- I'm afraid to.
- John wouldn't like it."

Exercise 2: Identifying Specific Limitations

In a similar manner, rephrase the exercise, this time specifying the thing you desire. For instance, "The reason I can't have a good job is..." Explore your thoughts and write them down.

After completing both exercises, take a moment of quiet reflection. Observe whether any of the thoughts resonate with you, even in the slightest. Acknowledge the limitations you may unwittingly impose upon yourself and your worldview.

Exercise 3: Unveiling Negative Attitudes

Compile a list of the most negative attitudes you can think of regarding yourself, others, relationships, the world, and life itself. Once again, sit in introspection and recognize which of these attitudes hold emotional sway over you, either consciously or subconsciously.

Should any emotions surface during these exercises, welcome them with complete acceptance. Embrace these feelings, allowing them to flow through you, understanding that they may connect to past experiences or early conditioning from influential figures in your life.

Exercise 4: Releasing and Replacing

As you sense the completion of this process, particularly if you've uncovered negative beliefs, symbolize your intent to release them by tearing up your lists and discarding them. This signifies your commitment to letting go of these limitations.

Now, in a state of relaxation and clarity, replace your constrictive beliefs with empowering empowerments. Here are a few suggestions:

- "I am now releasing my past."
- "I dissolve all negative, limiting beliefs."
- "I forgive and release everyone in my life."
- "I am naturally lovable and likable, no matter what."
- "I release all guilt, fears, resentment, and grudges."
- "I am free and clear!"
- "I love and appreciate myself."
- "Barriers to my full expression are dissolved."
- "The world is a beautiful place."
- "The universe always provides."

These empowerments serve as your bridge to transformation, gradually replacing self-imposed limitations with a newfound sense of liberation and positivity. This journey, rooted in ancient wisdom and enriched with modern insights, empowers you to unlock your fullest potential and embrace the abundant possibilities of life. Remember, the universe unfolds its mysteries to those who dare to explore their inner landscapes.

Liberating Through Forgiveness: A Path to Inner Harmony

In our journey of self-discovery and personal growth, forgiveness is a profound tool that can cleanse our souls and set us free. Inspired by the wisdom of ancient Indian scriptures, modern psychology, and the latest insights in self-transformation, we delve into clearing exercises that guide us towards forgiveness and release.

Exercise 1: Releasing Resentment and Anger

Begin by taking a piece of paper and writing down the names of individuals in your life who you believe have wronged you, harmed you, or caused you pain. Beside each name, jot down the specific actions or reasons for your resentment, anger, or hurt.

Now, close your eyes, find a moment of tranquility, and one by one, visualize these individuals. Engage in an internal dialogue with each one, expressing your past feelings of anger or hurt. However, make it clear that you are now committed to forgiving them for all transgressions. Offer them your blessing, saying, "I forgive you and release you. Go your own way and be happy."

Upon completing this process, write the affirmation, "I now forgive you and release you all," on your paper. Symbolically, dispose of the paper, signifying your willingness to let go of these burdensome past experiences.

This act of forgiveness is transformative, often relieving you of long-standing burdens of accumulated resentment. Remarkably, this energy of forgiveness can ripple through the lives of those involved, potentially bringing clarity and healing to their own journeys.

It's important to note that in some cases, especially with significant individuals like parents or spouses, forgiveness may not come easily in the initial attempt. If there's a deep emotional charge, consider seeking the guidance of a therapist or counselor or finding a safe space to express your emotions fully. The path to forgiveness begins with the acceptance and expression of your own feelings.

Exercise 2: Seeking Forgiveness from Others

Now, shift your focus to acknowledging instances where you believe you have caused harm or acted unjustly towards others. List the names of these individuals and specify your actions.

Once again, close your eyes, relax, and visualize each person individually. Confess your actions and ask for forgiveness, imagining them granting you their blessing. After completing this process, inscribe on your paper, "I forgive myself and absolve myself of all guilt, here and now, and forever!" Tear up the paper and discard it, symbolizing your release from self-blame and guilt.

These exercises in forgiveness hold the potential for miraculous healing, not only in terms of emotional well-being but also in addressing physical ailments often linked to accumulated anger and resentment. As you embark on this liberating journey, remember that forgiveness is a gift you give to yourself, a key to your own health and happiness.

Harmonizing Your Space: A Cleansing Ritual

In our quest for inner harmony and prosperity, it's essential to recognize the profound connection between our physical surroundings and our mental, emotional, and psychic well-being. In this final clearing process, we embark on a tangible journey to declutter and revitalize our living spaces, drawing inspiration from ancient Indian wisdom and modern principles of energy flow.

The Cleansing Ritual: A Physical and Symbolic Act

Begin by exploring every nook and cranny of your living space, from closets and drawers to basements and garages, identifying items that have accumulated over time and are no longer needed. This process mirrors the mental and emotional clearing you've been undergoing, making space for fresh energy to flow.

As you embark on this physical journey of decluttering, consider reciting empowerments to enhance the transformative power of this act:

1. "The more I outflow, the more space I create for good things to come to me."
2. "I love giving and I love receiving."
3. "As I clean up and clear out my physical space, I am cleaning up and clearing out my life in every way."
4. "I am now putting my life in order, preparing to accept all the good that is coming to me now."
5. "I give thanks now for all the good that I have and all the good things to come."

As you dispose of or donate unnecessary belongings, you're not just freeing up physical space but also symbolically purifying your mental and emotional realms. This act of conscious decluttering aligns with the age-old wisdom found in the Vedas and Upanishads, emphasizing the importance of order and harmony in one's environment as a reflection of inner peace.

The Profound Impact of Your Environment

Incorporating modern insights, we understand that our living spaces are not mere backgrounds but active participants in shaping our thoughts and emotions. Clutter and disarray in our physical surroundings can hinder the flow of positive energy, creating mental and emotional congestion.

By engaging in this cleansing ritual, you take proactive steps to invite abundance and prosperity into your life. This process signifies your readiness to accept all the good that is destined for you.

Furthermore, consider incorporating sustainable practices by recycling or donating items, aligning with the principles of responsible living and environmental consciousness. By doing so, you not only enhance your own well-being but also contribute to the well-being of the planet.

As you bask in the newfound clarity and spaciousness of your living environment, remember that this physical act of clearing echoes the deep spiritual journey you've undertaken. You are now prepared to welcome all the goodness that life has in store for you, embracing the principles of harmony, abundance, and gratitude from both ancient wisdom and modern knowledge.

Unlocking Your Potential: The Power of Empowerments and Clearing

In the pursuit of personal transformation, there exists a profound yet remarkably straightforward technique—a fusion of empowerments and clearing—that has yielded astonishing results for countless individuals. It is a practice that delves deep into the recesses of our consciousness, allowing us to challenge and reshape our beliefs. In this journey of self-discovery and empowerment, let us explore this technique, rooted in both timeless Indian wisdom and contemporary insights.

Empowerments: The Written Path to Transformation

Empowerments, the written expressions of our desires and beliefs, possess a unique potency. As we write them down, we engage both our creative and receptive faculties, amplifying their impact. This ancient practice finds resonance in modern psychology, demonstrating the profound influence of words on our thoughts and actions.

To embark on this transformative journey, select an affirmation that resonates with your aspirations. Then, write it repeatedly, ten or twenty times, on a sheet of paper. As you do, infuse each word with intention and understanding. Allow the affirmation's meaning to permeate your consciousness.

However, this process goes beyond mere repetition. Pay keen attention to your inner dialogue as you write. If doubts, resistance, or negative thoughts arise, embrace them as opportunities for deeper self-awareness. When this happens, turn the paper over, and on the reverse side, inscribe the opposing thoughts—the reasons why the affirmation appears unattainable or ineffective.

For instance, if your affirmation is "I am a successful singer and songwriter," and you encounter inner objections like "I'm not good enough" or "This won't work," transcribe these objections.

Clearing: The Pathway to Overcoming Limitations

The act of confronting and addressing these doubts and objections is the essence of clearing. It is here that we unearth the barriers within ourselves—often rooted in past experiences or limiting beliefs—that hinder our progress. This process aligns with the wisdom of the Vedas and Upanishads, which emphasize the importance of self-realization and the removal of mental and emotional obstacles.

With newfound clarity about your internal obstacles, craft empowerments that directly counteract these negative beliefs. For example, if you uncover a belief like "I can't be more successful than my father," counter it with an affirmation like "My father is proud and happy about my success."

Continue to write these empowerments diligently, ideally once or twice daily, for several days. As you engage with this practice, you not only challenge your limiting beliefs but also cultivate a sense of self-empowerment.

The Miraculous Unfolding

Through this process, you'll find that your empowerments often manifest surprisingly quickly after confronting your internal obstacles. Additionally, this practice serves as a gateway to profound self-insight, offering valuable glimpses into your own patterns and conditioning.

As you embark on this transformative journey, remember that you are not merely rewriting words on paper; you are rewriting the narrative of your life. Draw inspiration from the ancient wisdom of India, where self-realization and the removal of limitations have been foundational principles for centuries.

In the synergy of empowerments and clearing, you hold the key to unlock your true potential, ushering in a new chapter of empowerment, growth, and self-discovery.

Navigating Life's Path: Setting Clear Intentions and Goals

In the grand tapestry of life, perhaps one of the most intricate threads to weave is the art of discerning what we truly desire. The journey of self-discovery, coupled with the process of setting meaningful goals, forms the cornerstone of our aspirations. This exploration is akin to the quest for wisdom found in ancient Indian scriptures, where clarity of purpose is revered. Let us embark on this transformative voyage, drawing wisdom from the Vedas and contemporary insights.

The Journey to Clarity

In the intricate dance of existence, clarity of intention is paramount. It often emerges after traversing the labyrinth of confusion and uncertainty. This moment of revelation, where your desire becomes vividly evident, can be likened to a profound "click" in your consciousness—a sudden recognition of what you yearn for, accompanied by an unwavering belief that it is within your grasp.

Embrace the process of self-discovery with patience and self-compassion. Know that the path to clarity may meander through moments of confusion, despair, and hopelessness. These are the shadows that precede the dawn of understanding. Embrace them as integral to your growth.

An extraordinary example of this journey is my own decade-long odyssey towards finding my life partner. Beneath my conscious readiness lay layers of fear and ambivalence. Only when I confronted these emotions, acknowledging and healing them, did my intention crystallize. Three weeks later, I crossed paths with the man who would become my husband. This underscores that the darkest hour often precedes the dawn of clarity.

The Power of Goal Setting

The voyage of discovering your desires can be aided by the process of setting goals. Consider these exercises, which involve pen and paper, as valuable companions on your journey.

Firstly, remember that setting goals need not bind you to a rigid path. Goals are adaptable, evolving as you do. They are not mandates for exhaustive effort or relentless striving. Rather, they serve as guides, enhancing the flow of your creative energy, making life more effortless and enjoyable.

Approach the setting of goals as if life were an exhilarating game, one where achievement can bring deep fulfillment. Goals should be taken seriously enough to be valuable but lightly enough to maintain a sense of playfulness.

Overcoming Resistance and Embracing Change

As you embark on this journey, you may encounter emotional resistance. Feelings of despair, hopelessness, or the urge to distract yourself are not uncommon. These emotional reactions serve as signposts, revealing the ways in which you inadvertently thwart your own desires. Embrace these emotions, allow them to pass through you, and persist with the process. In facing them, you empower yourself.

Alternatively, you may relish this exploration, finding it expansive, enjoyable, and enlightening. Such a perspective is heartening and encouraged.

In conclusion, setting goals need not be complicated; simplicity often yields clarity. Begin with the straightforward and the obvious, knowing that you can refine and expand your goals along the way. Approach this journey with a spirit of curiosity, akin to the ancient sages who sought wisdom in the Vedas. Embrace the dance of life, where each goal is a step toward self-realization, and each aspiration a note in the symphony of your existence.

Charting Your Course: Goal-Setting and Manifestation

In the grand voyage of life, setting our sights on the horizon and plotting our course is an art that leads to profound transformation. It is akin to the ancient practice of yajna, where intentions are offered to the cosmic fire, and desires manifest as blessings. Let us embark on this transformative journey, blending timeless wisdom from the Vedas with modern insights.

Exploration of Desires

Begin by taking a moment to sit down with pen and paper. In the canvas of your life, sketch seven categories: Personal Growth/Education, Work/Career, Relationships, Creative Self-Expression, Money, Lifestyle/Possessions, and Leisure/Travel. Now, in the realm of your present life situation, jot down aspirations, changes, or improvements for each category. Don't overthink; let ideas flow freely like the sacred waters of the Ganges.

This exercise is a gentle nudge to stir your thoughts, igniting your contemplation about the desires nestled within the various facets of your life.

Painting Your Ideal Scene

Now, unfurl another blank canvas with the title "If I could be, do, and have everything I want, this would be my ideal scene." Within this canvas, recreate the same seven categories, and for each, paint a vibrant paragraph or two depicting your ideal life scenario. Allow your imagination to roam freely, unhindered by limitations.

This exercise is an invitation to transcend your current boundaries, embracing your wildest dreams. In this realm of boundless imagination, you can have everything your heart yearns for.

As you finish this artistic endeavor, add a category—World Situation/Environment. Paint a picture of the changes you wish to witness in the world, should you possess the power to bring transformation. Envision a world of harmony, where peace reigns, poverty fades, and humanity coexists with the Earth in reverence.

Read through your masterpiece and meditate upon it. Craft a mental tapestry of your ideal life in a harmonious world.

The Birth of Your Goals

Now, a fresh canvas beckons. Distill the essence of your ideal scene into a list of ten or twelve paramount life goals, as they resonate with you in this moment. Remember, these goals are not etched in stone; they can evolve and change over time.

Mapping the Next Five Years

Shift your focus to the canvas titled "My Five-year Goals." Here, articulate the most pivotal goals you aspire to achieve within the next five years. Phrase them as empowerments, as if they have already come to fruition. This lends strength to your intentions.

For instance: "I now own and reside on a serene twenty-acre estate, embraced by nature's beauty."

As you script your goals, ensure they align with your broader five-year vision. Each step should lead you closer to the grand tapestry of your dreams.

Progressing Step by Step

Return to the canvas with a shorter timeline, "My One-year Goals." Simplify your objectives; focus on the five or six most crucial. Ensure they harmonize with your overarching five-year goals. Let these goals be stepping stones, propelling you towards your desired destination.

Embrace the same process for six months, one month, and one week from now. Keep it succinct and meaningful. Align these short-term goals with your long-term vision, ensuring they contribute to your journey.

You may find envisioning events far into the future challenging, or you might feel uneasy about planning ahead. Remember, crafting a plan does not bind you to its course; life is ever-evolving. This exercise serves three purposes: practice in goal-setting, the acknowledgment of your fantasies' potential, and the illumination of your life's purpose and direction.

Keep this tapestry of goals in your notebook, revisiting and revising them periodically. Date each entry to trace the evolution of your aspirations. Your goals are living entities, growing as you do. Embrace this transformative journey with an open heart, guided by the wisdom of the Vedas and the endless possibilities of the cosmos.

Guiding Principles for Goal Setting: Nurturing Your Inner Garden

In the tapestry of life, setting and tending to our goals is akin to nurturing a flourishing garden. Allow me to impart timeless wisdom, melded with the essence of our Indian heritage, as we explore these guiding principles for your goal-setting journey.

1. Planting Seeds of Aspiration

As you embark on your journey, it's prudent to sow seeds that match the season. For short-term goals (ranging from a week to a month), simplicity and realism often yield fruitful results. Choose objectives you believe you can attain, unless the spirit of adventure beckons you towards a grander challenge. The horizon broadens with each step, unveiling new possibilities.

In the words of the Upanishads, "You are what your deep, driving desire is; as your desire is, so is your will; as your will is, so is your deed, and as your deed is, so is your destiny."

2. Embracing the Unfinished Symphony

In the symphony of life, missed notes are but pauses, not failures. When some goals remain unmet, resist the urge to chastise yourself or deem it as a defeat. Instead, acknowledge with clarity that a particular goal remains on the journey's horizon. Reflect upon whether it still resonates with your soul; if so, set it again. This graceful acknowledgment prevents these goals from festering in the shadows, keeping your path clear.

The teachings of the Bhagavad Gita echo this sentiment, "You have the right to perform your actions, but never to the fruits of your actions."

3. Celebrating Your Milestones

In your pursuit of aspirations, both great and small, pause to honor your achievements. Just as a lotus unfurls its petals in the morning sun, let your heart blossom with self-appreciation. Be mindful that every goal met, no matter how modest, deserves acknowledgment.

Savor this wisdom from the Mahabharata, "Success is never final, and failure is never fatal. It's courage that counts."

4. Balancing the Scales of Ambition

Guard against spreading yourself too thin. Set goals that resonate deeply with your being. Should feelings of overwhelm, confusion, or despondency arise, simplify your objectives. Consider focusing on a singular aspect of your life, such as your career or relationships. The aim is to derive joy from life's journey, not to burden your path.

In the spirit of Vedantic wisdom, "You are what your deep, driving desire is." Set intentions aligned with your true desires.

5. Seeking Support When Needed

Should you consistently encounter obstacles on your path to realization, it may be time to seek guidance. Unseen barriers may hinder your progress. In such moments, consider the wisdom of seeking therapy or a supportive community to aid in your emotional healing.

Remember, as the Rigveda suggests, "The good have the power to overcome obstacles." Seek help when required; it's a sign of inner strength.

6. Timing and Trust

Lastly, acknowledge that life has its rhythms. There is a time for setting goals and a time for letting them flow naturally with the current of your life. Trust in the universal flow, guided by the wisdom of the cosmos.

In the words of the Upanishads, "You are what your deep, driving desire is." Allow your desires to merge seamlessly with the river of life.

As you navigate the labyrinth of goals, let these principles be your North Star, guiding you towards a life well-lived. Embrace the teachings of our ancient sages, and may your aspirations flourish like vibrant petals in the garden of existence.

Harnessing the Power of Pioneering Thinking: Weaving Your Dreams

In the realm of manifesting one's desires, the art of Pioneering Thinking stands as a potent tool. It assumes various forms—mental imagery, spoken or written words, or even physical images, akin to the ancient concept of 'Yantras.' To embark on this journey, let us blend the wisdom of the Vedas and Upanishads with contemporary insights, enveloped in narratives from the heart of India.

1. The Artistry of Written Empowerments

Pioneering Thinking can take root through the written word. The act of crystallizing your desires on paper not only imparts clarity but also sets the wheels of manifestation in motion. Consider this exercise, a cherished gem of wisdom:

Begin with a Goal: Choose a goal that resonates deeply within you, whether it's a grand vision or a modest aspiration. Write it down succinctly in a single sentence.

Paint Your Ideal Scene: Below your goal, inscribe "Ideal Scene." This is where the magic unfolds. Describe, in vivid detail, how your life would look once your goal is fully realized. Pen it in the present tense, as though it already dances in the canvas of reality. Allow your imagination to run wild, crafting a scene of utmost perfection.

Affirmation of Manifestation: Conclude your narrative with the words, "This, or something better, is now manifesting for me in totally satisfying and harmonious ways, for the highest good of all concerned." Add any other empowerments that resonate with your soul, and sign your name, imprinting your commitment to this vision.

Meditative Embodiment: In the tranquil embrace of meditation, revisit your ideal scene. Visualize it with unwavering belief as you recite your empowerments. This union of intention and imagery harmonizes your desires with the cosmos.

2. Treasuring Your Dreams

Once crafted, your ideal scene becomes a precious treasure. Keep it close, in your notebook, on your desk, or near your bedside. Let it breathe life into your everyday existence. Revisit it frequently, making refinements as the tides of life evolve.

Yet, heed this sage advice. Should you tuck it away and forget, the universe often conspires to bring your desires to fruition, even without your conscious effort. The ancient Vedas speak of the interconnectedness of all things; your intentions, once set, ripple through the cosmic web.

The Tale of Manifestation

Allow me to share a story deeply rooted in the Indian soil, where Pioneering Thinking is woven into the cultural fabric. In the ancient city of Varanasi, there lived a humble weaver named Raj. Despite his modest means, Raj harbored a dream—to educate his children and elevate their lives.

Every night, Raj would retire to his loom, pausing to gaze at a piece of parchment on which he had penned his aspirations. His ideal scene depicted his children clad in graduation gowns, adorned with smiles that radiated wisdom. Raj would close his eyes, visualize their academic success, and whisper empowerments into the cosmic tapestry.

Years passed, and Raj's children grew. Through unwavering determination and their father's boundless faith, they graduated from prestigious universities, living the very ideal scene etched in their hearts.

Embrace Your Inner Weaver

In the grand tapestry of life, you are the weaver of your destiny. The Vedas teach us, "You are what your deep, driving desire is." Allow your desires to find expression through Pioneering Thinking, knowing that your intentions, nurtured with dedication, shall manifest in the symphony of existence.

As you embark on this voyage, remember that the universe dances to the melody of your heart's desires. May your ideal scenes flourish like vibrant yantras, drawing forth the colors of your dreams onto the canvas of reality.

Charting Your Destiny: The Art of Treasure Mapping

In the intricate tapestry of manifesting your desires, the age-old tradition of creating a "treasure map" stands as a beacon of both power and delight. Drawing from the essence of India's vibrant culture, enriched with ancient wisdom and contemporary insight, we embark on a journey to craft your destiny in the most artistic way.

1. The Marvel of Treasure Maps

A treasure map is your tangible conduit to your envisioned reality, akin to the sacred yantras that grace Indian spiritual traditions. It possesses a unique ability to crystallize your desires into a vivid and compelling image, acting as a blueprint for the universe to follow. Much like the architectural plans of a grand temple, your treasure map guides the cosmic forces toward your goal.

Creating a treasure map can take various forms: drawing, painting, or crafting a collage from images and words found in magazines, books, or photographs. Rest assured, artistic prowess is not a prerequisite; even a simple, childlike treasure map can work wonders.

2. Navigating the Treasure Map

To maximize the effectiveness of your treasure map, consider these guiding principles:

Focused Intent: Devote each treasure map to a single goal or aspect of your life. This clarity of purpose allows your mind to concentrate its energies more precisely. Craft individual maps for your relationships, career, spiritual growth, and other facets of life.

Dimensions of Desire: Choose a size that resonates with you—whether it's a page in your notebook, a wall-mounted masterpiece, or a pocket-sized token. Materials like light cardboard can ensure its longevity.

You in the Picture: Place yourself at the heart of your treasure map. For added realism, use a photograph or a drawn representation. Witness yourself being, doing, or having your cherished objective. Whether you're globe-trotting, adorned in new attire, or the proud author of a book, portray your ideal self.

The Vision of Completion: Depict your desired situation in its perfected state, as though it already exists. There's no need to outline the "how" of its manifestation; focus solely on the finished masterpiece. Exclude any hints of negativity or undesirable elements.

Vibrant Palette: Splash your treasure map with vibrant colors. This kaleidoscope enriches its influence on your consciousness, infusing it with vitality.

Believable Reality: Craft a setting that feels believable to you. Immerse yourself in a scenario that resonates with your inner truth.

The Symbol of the Infinite: Include a symbol that holds profound significance for you—an "Om" sign, a cross, figures like Christ or Buddha, or even a radiant sun embodying universal intelligence. This symbol acknowledges the boundless source from which all creation emanates.

Empowerments' Embrace: Enhance your treasure map with empowerments. Convey your desires in words like, "Here I am driving my new hybrid gas and electric car." Remember to incorporate the cosmic affirmation, "This, or something better, now manifests for me in totally satisfying and harmonious ways, for the highest good of all concerned."

Breathing Life into Your Map

The creation of your treasure map is a significant step towards the manifestation of your dreams. Dedicate a few minutes each day to gaze upon it in quiet contemplation. Throughout your day, let it occupy your thoughts sporadically. This simple practice aligns your consciousness with your vision.

In the heart of India's spiritual tapestry, your treasure map is your yantra—a sacred symbol of your desires. As you delve into this creative process, remember that the universe awaits your artistic command. With your treasure map as the compass, embark on the voyage to manifest your dreams and witness your desires materialize in the grand canvas of life.

Crafting Your Vision: A Gallery of Treasure Map Ideas

In the vibrant tapestry of manifestation, treasure maps stand as artistic gateways to your deepest desires. Drawing inspiration from India's rich cultural canvas and blending ancient wisdom with modern insights, let's embark on a creative journey to tailor your treasure map, complete with quotes, names, and stories that resonate with our Indian ethos.

1. Nurturing Your Well-Being: A Treasure Map for Health

Picture yourself in a state of radiant health, engaged in activities that symbolize your vitality. Craft a scene where you exude health, and life flows through you like the sacred Ganges. Embrace the wisdom of Ayurveda and Yoga, for they hold the keys to holistic well-being. As the Bhagavad Gita proclaims, "You have the right to perform your prescribed duties, but you are not entitled to the fruits of your actions."

2. The Journey to Your Ideal Physique: Mapping Weight and Physical Wellness

Visualize your perfect body, a vessel of strength and confidence. Paste a picture of a body resembling your ideal physique and crown it with your own head—a visual mantra of your aspirations. Channel the essence of Lord Hanuman's devotion and dedication to sculpt your physical temple. As you affirm, "I feel wonderful and look fantastic now that I weigh 125 pounds, and am in great physical condition," remember the words of Swami Vivekananda, "Arise, awake, and stop not until the goal is achieved."

3. The Mirror of Self-Image and Beauty: Reflecting Your Inner Radiance

Craft an image that mirrors your self-love and beauty, reflecting the divine within. Embrace the timeless wisdom of inner beauty celebrated in the Upanishads: "The self is the sun shining in the sky; he is the air that fills the world, and the fire here in the heart. He is the truth; he is the soul." Surround your self-image with symbols of warmth, love, and relaxation, echoing the teachings of Buddha on inner peace.

4. Nurturing Relationships: A Tapestry of Love

Envision harmonious relationships with loved ones, family, and friends. Place photographs, symbols, and empowerments on your treasure map to depict joyful connections, heartfelt communication, and profound love. Let the essence of Mahatma Gandhi's words resonate: "You must be the change you want to see in the world."

5. Crafting Your Ideal Career: The Professional Odyssey

Picture yourself in a career that resonates with your heart's desires. Envision a fulfilling job with colleagues who inspire you. Be specific about your earnings, location, and job satisfaction. As you do so, remember the words of Swami Vivekananda: "Take up one idea. Make that one idea your life; dream of it; think of it; live on that idea."

6. Unleashing Creativity: An Artistic Voyage

Stimulate your creative energies by using symbols, colors, and images that signify the blossoming of your artistic expression. Showcase yourself manifesting captivating and imaginative creations, igniting your inner genius. Channel the spirit of Rabindranath Tagore, who proclaimed, "You can't cross the sea merely by standing and staring at the water."

7. The Tapestry of Harmonious Relationships: Family and Friends

Craft a vision of your family and friends immersed in harmonious, loving relationships, radiating joy and unity. Celebrate the bonds that bind us, drawing from the teachings of ancient Indian scriptures that emphasize the importance of relationships. As the Bhagavad Gita reminds us, "He who is not envious but is a kind friend to all living entities, who does not think himself a proprietor, who is free from false ego and equal both in happiness and distress, he is very dear to Me."

8. Wanderlust: A Journey of Exploration

Embark on a visual adventure by placing yourself in your dream travel destinations. Visualize abundant time and resources to savor every moment of your journeys. Draw inspiration from the travel tales of Swami Vivekananda and explore the world with an open heart.

These are but a few brushstrokes on the canvas of your treasure map. Let your imagination run free and add layers of dreams, desires, and aspirations. Revel in the creation process, for in your treasure map, you hold the brush to paint your destiny. As you revisit this masterpiece daily, remember the words of Swami Sivananda: "Put your heart, mind, and soul into even your smallest acts. This is the secret of success."

Harmony of Health and Beauty: A Journey Through Pioneering Thinking

In the vibrant tapestry of Indian life, the pursuit of health and beauty has been an age-old endeavor. Just as the lotus blooms in muddy waters, our well-being and allure can blossom through the art of Pioneering Thinking. In the embrace of our rich heritage and wisdom, let us explore how transforming our mental and emotional landscape can profoundly impact our physical vitality and grace.

1. Treasure Maps: Charting the Course to Wellness

Much like the sacred yantras that grace our temples, treasure maps serve as celestial navigators of our aspirations. Craft a treasure map tailored to your health and beauty goals, adorned with vibrant hues and sacred symbols. In the spirit of Ayurveda, the map becomes your personal "Rasaayana," a path to rejuvenation and longevity.

2. Physical Exercise: A Divine Dance of Strength

Physical exercise, be it the rhythmic beat of a jog or the graceful asanas of yoga, is a divine dance of strength. Infuse this dance with the power of Pioneering Thinking. While running, visualize yourself gliding effortlessly, akin to Lord Krishna's divine dance, covering vast distances with each stride. During moments of meditation, affirm your growing strength, aligning with the belief that you daily become swifter and more resilient. Embrace the spirit of "Bhagavad Gita," where Lord Krishna imparts wisdom on the path of action and discipline.

3. Dance and Yoga: Embodied Elegance

Dance and yoga, ancient arts of self-expression, invite us to embody elegance and flexibility. As you gracefully move through these practices, visualize your muscles relaxing and stretching, your body becoming a vessel of flexibility and poise. Channel the teachings of Bharata Muni's "Natya Shastra," where dance is a manifestation of divinity, and Patanjali's Yoga Sutras, which guide us toward balance and unity.

4. Sporting Excellence: Pursuit of Victory

For sports enthusiasts, visualize excellence in your chosen field. Picture yourself achieving victories and breaking records, much like our revered sports icons. As you visualize, remember the legacy of our cricket legends and Olympic heroes, who inspire us to reach for greatness.

5. Holistic Well-being: Mind, Body, and Soul

Incorporate holistic well-being into your willpowers. Envision a harmonious union of mind, body, and soul, echoing the Upanishadic wisdom, "Tat Tvam Asi" - You are that. Cultivate the oneness of your physical and mental aspects, nurturing your entire being.

As you embark on this transformative journey, sculpting your reality through Pioneering Thinking, remember the profound words of the Vedas: "Sarve Bhavantu Sukhinah, Sarve Santu Niramayah" - May all be happy, may all be free from illness. Your health and beauty are not mere reflections in the mirror but a manifestation of your inner world. Through the art of Pioneering Thinking, you become the artist, shaping your masterpiece with the colors of your thoughts and emotions. Your journey is a hymn to wellness and beauty, a testament to the ancient wisdom that flows through the veins of our culture.

The Art of Inner Beauty and Wellness: An Indian Perspective

In the colorful tapestry of Indian culture, beauty is not merely skin deep; it is a reflection of inner harmony and well-being. Embracing the wisdom of our heritage, let us delve into practices that nurture both body and soul, transforming daily routines into sacred rituals.

1. Beauty Treatments as Rituals

In the sacred sanctuaries of our homes, daily beauty rituals become more than mundane tasks—they are pathways to self-love. Imagine, as you indulge in a hot bath, the warm water enveloping you like the healing touch of Lord Dhanvantari, the divine physician. Visualize your worries dissolving, leaving behind your innate radiance. As you apply lotion or oil, let it be an act of self-affirmation, your skin responding with newfound smoothness and beauty. Each stroke of the brush becomes a mantra, affirming the strength and beauty of your teeth. In these moments, you channel the teachings of Ayurveda, where self-care is an offering to the divine residing within.

2. Eating Mindfully: The Alchemy of Nourishment

Food is not just sustenance; it is an alchemical process that transmutes universal energy into life force within us. Yet, many of us eat unconsciously, plagued by fears of weight gain and illness. Let us redefine our relationship with food through a daily ritual. Before each meal, close your eyes and express gratitude to the universe for this sustenance. Acknowledge the interconnectedness of all beings who played a role in bringing this meal to your plate. Open your eyes, observe the colors and aromas, and savor each bite with mindfulness. Speak silently to your food, affirming that it transforms into life energy, enhancing your health and beauty. This practice aligns with the principle of "Prana," the vital life force, in our food.

3. The Elixir of Life: Water Ritual

Water, the elixir of life, has the power to rejuvenate. As you pour a glass of cool water, imagine it as the sacred "Amrit," the nectar of immortality. With each sip, visualize impurities being washed away, replaced by energy, vitality, beauty, and health. This simple act resonates with the sacred rivers of India, revered for their purifying properties. Water, when honored, becomes a source of renewal.

4. Empowerments for Inner and Outer Radiance

Empowerments are like mantras that echo within, shaping our reality. As you gaze upon your reflection, repeat empowerments rooted in self-love and empowerment. Embrace your journey to greater health and beauty. In the realm of your thoughts, envision yourself as slender, strong, and in perfect harmony with your body. Declare your desire to nourish your body with foods that serve its highest good. With each affirmation, you awaken the power of "Shakti," the divine feminine energy that resides within us all.

5. The Beauty Within

In the mosaic of your existence, remember that beauty is a reflection of your inner world. As you cultivate self-love and appreciation, you become naturally attractive, drawing others to your inner light. Your body is a temple, a sacred vessel that carries the essence of your being. Love and honor it as it is, for in doing so, you manifest the essence of true Indian beauty—inner radiance that transcends time.

As you embark on this transformative journey, weaving ancient wisdom with modern understanding, you become the architect of your own beauty. With each ritual, affirmation, and mindful act, you paint a canvas of wellness and radiance that celebrates the tapestry of your existence. In the words of the Upanishads, "Tat Tvam Asi"—You are that divine beauty, waiting to be unveiled.

Group Pioneering Thinking: A Collective Journey Towards Manifestation

In the diverse tapestry of India's spiritual heritage, the practice of group Pioneering Thinking finds a profound resonance. Drawing inspiration from our ancient scriptures, the Vedas and Upanishads, and incorporating contemporary wisdom and technology, we embark on a transformative exploration of the power of collective willpower.

1. The Synergy of Group Energy

In the sacred land where spiritual gatherings have thrived for millennia, the concept of collective willpower transcends individual boundaries. It is a beacon of unity, where the energy of each participant harmoniously merges with the whole. As the Rigveda proclaims, "Ekam sad vipra bahudha vadanti," meaning "Truth is one, but the wise speak it in many ways." In this unity, we discover the essence of collective Pioneering Thinking.

2. Group Dynamics: Amplifying Intentions

Be it within the sanctified walls of a temple, the serene ambiance of a yoga class, or the vibrant atmosphere of a community gathering, the power of collective willpower amplifies intentions. Like the diverse threads of a tapestry converging to create a masterpiece, individual energies unite to manifest shared goals. In the spirit of "Sangha," where like-minded individuals come together in pursuit of a common purpose, group Pioneering Thinking comes to life.

3. The Healing Circle: A Harmonious Convergence

One of the most profound applications of collective willpower is witnessed in healing circles. Drawing from the holistic principles of Ayurveda, participants collectively channel healing energies. Guided by the belief in the interconnectedness of all beings, these circles become a conduit for universal healing energy. As the Upanishads affirm, "Tat Tvam Asi," meaning "You are that," reflecting the inherent unity of all existence.

4. Musical Harmony: Singing and Chanting

In the realm of music, which has always played a pivotal role in our spiritual gatherings, songs and chants become vehicles for collective intention. Just as the rhythms of the tabla and the melodies of the sitar resonate in unison, so do the voices of a group singing or chanting in harmony. Through these melodious vibrations, intentions are magnified, echoing the sentiments of our ancient verses.

5. Meditative Willpower: A Collective Journey Within

Within the stillness of a meditation circle, participants embark on a collective journey within. Inspired by the teachings of yogic practices, they visualize and affirm shared goals. The words of the Bhagavad Gita, where Lord Krishna imparts wisdom to Arjuna, remind us that our collective thoughts possess immense power. In these moments of shared silence, we tap into the reservoir of collective consciousness.

6. Treasure Mapping: A Shared Vision

The art of treasure mapping takes on a new dimension within a group. Whether it is a family, a workgroup, or a spiritual community, each member contributes to the creation of a shared treasure map. Guided by the principle of "Vasudhaiva Kutumbakam," the world is one family, the collective willpower on the map embodies the aspirations of all. It is a testament to the strength of unity in diversity.

7. Empowerments in Unison: The Power of the Spoken Word

Empowerments, when spoken collectively, resonate with potent energy. Partners within the group engage in affirmative dialogue, reinforcing each other's intentions. The words "Om Shanti," symbolizing peace, echo through the room, embodying the spirit of "Lokah Samastah Sukhino Bhavantu," may all beings be happy and free.

8. The Digital Sangha: Harnessing Technology

In the digital age, technology acts as a bridge, connecting individuals across geographical boundaries. Online forums, guided meditation apps, and virtual gatherings enable people to engage in collective willpower effortlessly. Through the fusion of tradition and technology, a global Sangha is formed, where collective intentions ripple across the digital realm.

9. Stories of Unity: From Samudra Manthan to Modern Endeavors

As we traverse this path of collective willpower, our history and mythology offer timeless stories of unity. From the churning of the cosmic ocean, Samudra Manthan, where Devas and Asuras united to obtain the nectar of immortality, to the modern-day success stories of Indian start-ups emerging as global leaders through collective vision and effort, our heritage reflects the enduring power of collective intent.

In conclusion, group Pioneering Thinking is a sacred thread that weaves through the fabric of Indian culture. It is an embodiment of our timeless wisdom, a reflection of our spiritual gatherings, and a testament to the potential of collective intention. As we converge our energies and intentions, we manifest the truth of "Ekam Sat," the one truth, collectively and harmoniously.

Harmonious Relationships Through Pioneering Thinking: Nurturing the Bonds of Unity

In the vibrant tapestry of Indian culture, the quest for harmonious relationships has always been deeply rooted. Drawing from our timeless wisdom, the Vedas and Upanishads, and merging it with contemporary insights and technology, we embark on a transformative journey of enhancing our relationships through the profound practice of Pioneering Thinking.

1. The Mirror of Relationships: A Reflection of Beliefs

As human beings, our connections with one another are a sacred dance of energies. Our thoughts and beliefs about each other shape the quality of our relationships. In the words of the ancient sages, "Yat pinde tat brahmande," meaning "As is the individual, so is the universe." Our relationships are mirrors that reflect our inner world.

2. The Power of Intent: Manifesting Our Deepest Beliefs

In the intricate tapestry of human relationships, our intentions hold the key. Our expectations, beliefs, and subconscious desires shape the dynamics of our connections. Just as Lord Krishna guided Arjuna on the battlefield of Kurukshetra in the Bhagavad Gita, we must recognize our responsibility in co-creating our relationships.

3. Embracing Responsibility: The First Step to Transformation

Taking an attitude of complete responsibility for our relationships is akin to invoking the teachings of Lord Shiva, the transformer. Regardless of appearances, we acknowledge that we play a significant role in shaping our connections. This shift empowers us to unravel the layers of our beliefs and intentions.

4. Unmasking Limiting Beliefs: The Clearing Process

To unearth our limiting beliefs, we embark on a journey of introspection. Inspired by the profound Upanishadic mantra "Tat Tvam Asi," meaning "You are that," we explore the beliefs that hinder our relationships. Through writing and reflection, we uncover the thought patterns that no longer serve us.

5. The Transformative Power of Empowerments

In the spirit of empowerments, we embrace the practice of speaking positive truths into our relationships. Much like the sacred chant of "Om Shanti," we utter empowerments that nourish our connections. Instead of dwelling on shortcomings, we affirm growth and improvement, transforming our relationships from within.

6. Pioneering Thinking: Shaping Harmonious Bonds

Pioneering Thinking becomes our guiding light in reshaping relationships. Drawing inspiration from the concept of "Lokah Samastah Sukhino Bhavantu," may all beings be happy and free, we envision the harmonious dynamics we seek. Through willpower, we mend the threads of connection and pave the way for unity.

7. Healing Through Willpower: A Harmonious Convergence

Just as Ayurveda seeks balance and harmony, we channel the healing energies of willpower. In a circle of mutual intent, participants visualize collective healing, guided by the principle of interconnectedness. The circle becomes a vessel for universal healing, mirroring the philosophy of "Vasudhaiva Kutumbakam," the world is one family.

8. Stories of Transformation: From Ancient Myths to Modern Realities

In our journey to enrich relationships, we draw from timeless tales of transformation. From the churning of the cosmic ocean, Samudra Manthan, where Devas and Asuras united to attain the nectar of immortality, to modern narratives of individuals and couples rekindling their bonds through Pioneering Thinking, our heritage speaks of the enduring potential for growth.

In conclusion, the practice of Pioneering Thinking offers us a profound path to nurturing harmonious relationships. It is a reflection of our timeless wisdom, a bridge between our beliefs and our connections, and a testament to our ability to shape the dynamics of unity. As we embark on this transformative journey, we heed the wisdom of the Vedas and Upanishads, recognizing that our relationships are a sacred mirror, inviting us to evolve and unite.

Part 5

Divine Expression: Unleashing Creativity for Manifestation

In the tapestry of life, the essence of successful manifestation lies not only in the tangible but in the transformation of consciousness. These profound words echo the wisdom of our ancient scriptures, connecting us with the eternal truths of the Vedas and Upanishads. Let us embark on a journey of creative living, guided by the divine wisdom that transcends time and space.

1. The Divine Manifestation Within: Unveiling the Eternal Truth

As we delve into the art of living creatively, we are reminded of the quintessential truth from the Upanishads: "Aham Brahmasmi," meaning "I am Brahman." This ancient mantra encapsulates the essence of divine manifestation within every individual. Creative living is the path to manifesting the divine that resides within us.

2. The Power of Conscious Transformation: A Shift in Perception

In the quest for creative living, we recognize that true manifestation goes beyond mere external forms. It is a sacred dance of unveiling the divine essence within and seeing it reflected in the world. This shift in consciousness aligns with the profound concept of "Tat Tvam Asi," meaning "You are that," where the individual realizes their unity with the divine.

3. The Creative Force of Change: Nurturing Growth

David Spangle's words resonate with the ancient principle of "Lila," the divine play of creation. True success in manifestation lies not in stagnant outcomes but in the dynamic dance of growth and transformation. Creative living is a testament to our ability to co-create with the divine and bring forth a more complete revelation of God.

4. The Art of Creative Manifestation: Blending Tradition and Innovation

In our pursuit of creative living, we harmonize tradition with innovation. Just as Lord Brahma, the creator in Hindu cosmology, continuously creates and recreates the universe, we too engage in the ongoing process of manifestation. Drawing from the wisdom of our ancestors, we infuse it with modern insights and technology to shape our reality.

5. Stories of Divine Manifestation: From Mythology to Modernity

Our rich heritage is replete with stories of divine manifestation. From the birth of Lord Ganesha to the churning of the cosmic ocean, these narratives inspire us to tap into our creative potential. In contemporary times, individuals manifest the divine through acts of compassion, innovation, and unity, demonstrating that the divine is ever-present in our lives.

6. Creative Living in the Modern Age: Embracing Conscious Evolution

In the digital age, the art of creative living takes on new dimensions. We harness the power of technology, echoing the principle of "Neti, Neti" from the Upanishads, meaning "Not this, not this." We transcend limitations and explore boundless possibilities, aligning our creativity with the infinite.

7. The Wisdom of the Vedas and Upanishads: Guiding Our Path

As we navigate the realm of creative living, we draw wisdom from the Vedas and Upanishads, where ancient sages contemplated the nature of reality and consciousness. Their insights continue to illuminate our journey, reminding us that manifestation is a sacred act of unveiling the divine within and without.

In conclusion, creative living is a sacred endeavor that harmonizes the ancient wisdom of our scriptures with the dynamism of the modern world. It is an ode to the divine manifestation within us, a testament to our capacity to co-create with the cosmos. As we embrace creative living, we embody the eternal truth that every manifestation is a revelation of the divine, and every moment is an opportunity to manifest God more fully.

The Essence of Creative Consciousness: Unleashing Divine Potential

Creative consciousness is not a mere practice; it is the very essence of our existence. It beckons us to recognize that we are not separate from the divine; we are divine manifestations, co-creators of the cosmos, and stewards of our own reality. In this profound journey, let us explore the depths of creative consciousness, drawing inspiration from the wisdom of the Vedas and Upanishads.

1. The Divine Connection: Oneness with the Cosmos

The ancient Vedas proclaim, "Aham Brahmasmi," echoing the truth that "I am Brahman." Creative consciousness invites us to realize our inseparable connection with the divine. We are not isolated beings striving for abundance; we are divine reflections endowed with limitless potential.

2. The Power of Co-Creation: Taking Responsibility

In the realm of creative consciousness, we bear witness to our role as co-creators of the universe. We accept responsibility for every facet of our reality. The divine spark within us ignites the creative process, and we embrace our ability to shape our world.

3. Beyond Scarcity: Embracing Abundance

As we journey deeper into creative consciousness, the illusion of lack and scarcity dissipates. The Upanishads teach us, "Tat Tvam Asi," signifying "You are that." We recognize that there is no need to chase external achievements; our inner reservoir holds the potential for everything.

4. The Divine Potential Within: Unveiling the Creator

Each of us embodies the creative principle, mirroring the cosmic dance of Lord Brahma. Within us lies the potential to manifest divine qualities and shape our reality. We are not mere spectators; we are active participants in the grand tapestry of creation.

5. Stories of Divine Manifestation: From Mythology to Reality

Our heritage is replete with stories of divine manifestation. Just as Lord Ganesha's birth symbolizes creativity, we too have the power to birth new ideas and innovations. Modern legends arise from acts of compassion and unity, affirming that divine potential is ever-present in our lives.

6. Creative Consciousness in the Modern Age: Bridging Tradition and Innovation

In the digital era, creative consciousness finds expression through technology and innovation. We align with the principle of "Neti, Neti" ("Not this, not this") by transcending limitations and exploring uncharted realms of creativity. The fusion of ancient wisdom with modern tools propels us forward.

7. The Wisdom of the Vedas and Upanishads: Guiding Light

As we delve into the depths of creative consciousness, we draw wisdom from the Vedas and Upanishads, where sages contemplated the nature of existence. Their teachings remind us that creative manifestation is an act of realizing our divine potential and making it tangible in the physical realm.

In conclusion, creative consciousness is the tapestry that weaves together ancient truths and modern realities. It is an awakening to our divine nature, an acknowledgment of our co-creative prowess, and a celebration of abundance within. As we embrace creative consciousness, we embody the eternal truth that we are the architects of our universe, guided by the divine spark within us.

Unveiling Your Divine Purpose: Illuminating the Path

In the tapestry of existence, every individual possesses an innate longing to make a meaningful contribution to the world, to uplift fellow beings, and to savor the richness of personal fulfillment. Our lives are the canvas upon which we paint our unique stories, leaving indelible marks of inspiration. As we embark on this transformative journey, let us draw wisdom from the timeless Vedas and Upanishads, merging ancient insights with modern understanding.

1. The Essence of Human Existence: Serving a Higher Calling

The ancient sages proclaimed, "Vasudhaiva Kutumbakam," translating to "The world is one family." At the core of our being lies a deep-seated yearning to create a positive impact on our global family. It is a profound understanding that our own joy is intrinsically linked to the joy we bring to others.

2. Unveiling Your Unique Offering: Your Higher Purpose

Within each soul resides a magnificent purpose, a sacred duty waiting to be unveiled. This purpose is not elusive but deeply ingrained in our essence. It beckons us to align our actions with our true selves, expressing our innate gifts and passions. Our higher purpose is the compass guiding us on our life's voyage.

3. Embracing Authenticity: Being Your True Self

In the journey of discovering our higher purpose, authenticity is the North Star. We must wholeheartedly embrace our true selves, for it is from this wellspring of authenticity that our unique contributions flow effortlessly. The Vedas remind us, "Satyam eva jayate," emphasizing the triumph of truth.

4. Pioneering Thinking: A Gateway to Clarity

Pioneering Thinking serves as a powerful tool for unraveling the tapestry of our higher purpose. Through introspection and willpower, we illuminate the recurring themes in our dreams, aspirations, and endeavors. These patterns offer profound insights into our life's deeper meaning.

5. Manifesting Your Purpose: Harmony with the Universe

As we strive to manifest our desires, we must remain attuned to our higher purpose. If our manifestations do not align with our soul's calling, we may encounter resistance. Patience and inner guidance are our allies on this path. Trust that the universe orchestrates every step of our journey.

6. A Time of Transformation: Your Role in the Cosmic Symphony

Our planet is undergoing a profound transformation. Each individual plays a vital role simply by embracing their authentic selves. By doing so, we become conduits for positive change, weaving our unique threads into the cosmic tapestry. The Upanishads echo, "Tat Tvam Asi," signifying "You are that." We are the instruments of transformation.

7. Stories of Purpose: Inspiration from Legends

Throughout history, individuals have heeded their higher calling and left an indelible mark on humanity. From the wisdom of Mahatma Gandhi's non-violence to the innovation of Dr. APJ Abdul Kalam, their lives inspire us to discover and live our own higher purpose.

In conclusion, the journey of unveiling our higher purpose is a sacred quest. It is an odyssey of self-discovery, authenticity, and service to humanity. As we align with our unique calling, we become torchbearers of positive change in this time of cosmic transformation. Let us heed the wisdom of the ancients and the spirit of modernity, and together, we shall co-create a world enriched by purpose and compassion.

Crafting the Masterpiece of Your Life: An Artistic Odyssey

In the grand tapestry of existence, each of us dons the mantle of an artist, and life itself becomes our most exquisite masterpiece. Every passing moment is akin to a stroke of the brush, bearing within it boundless potential and infinite horizons. As we embark on this artistic journey, let us draw inspiration from the profound wisdom of the Vedas and Upanishads, seamlessly blending ancient insights with contemporary understanding.

1. The Artist Within: Embracing Your Creative Essence

Deep within our souls lies the artist, waiting to express itself. In the words of the Upanishads, "Aham Brahmasmi" reminds us, "I am the Infinite Reality." We are creators of our destinies, endowed with the power to shape our lives into magnificent works of art.

2. A Canvas of Infinite Choices: Exploring New Horizons

Each moment unveils a canvas of choices, a myriad of paths to traverse. We possess the agency to perpetuate the status quo or to embark on new and uncharted journeys, filled with the promise of growth and fulfillment. Our lives are the quintessential playground of possibilities.

3. The Artist's Palette: A Spectrum of Opportunities

Life, like an artist's palette, offers a spectrum of colors and hues. We can choose to paint our lives with the same strokes, or we can experiment with novel and vibrant shades, potentially leading to more enriching experiences. The Vedas emphasize, "Satyam eva jayate," underscoring the triumph of truth and authenticity.

4. The Art of Decision-Making: A Profound Game

The unfolding of life is akin to a captivating game, where each moment presents an opportunity and a choice. We engage in this delightful dance of decisions, sculpting our destinies with every mindful step. The game is not merely about existence; it's an extraordinary art form.

5. The Infinite Canvas: A Continual Journey

Life's canvas knows no bounds, stretching into eternity. Our artistic journey is not confined by time or space. With each stroke of creativity, we contribute to the evolving tapestry of humanity, echoing the timeless wisdom of the Vedas: "Tat Tvam Asi," signifying "You are that."

6. The Artistic Anecdotes: Narratives of Inspiration

Throughout history, countless artists have left indelible imprints on the canvas of time. Be it the Pioneering artistry of Raja Ravi Varma or the musical genius of A.R. Rahman, their lives and works inspire us to explore the depths of our own creative potential.

In conclusion, life itself is an art form—a masterpiece waiting to be sculpted. We are the artists, and our choices, the brushstrokes that define our existence. Let us draw inspiration from the ancients and the spirit of modernity, fusing their wisdom into our creative journeys. As we paint the canvas of our lives with authenticity, courage, and innovation, we contribute to the ever-evolving narrative of human existence. In the grand gallery of life, let our masterpieces shine as beacons of inspiration for generations to come.

Gratitude: Nurturing the Garden of Inspiration

In the vibrant garden of life, where wisdom and inspiration bloom in abundance, I am deeply grateful to those whose support and love have nurtured these blossoms. Inspired by the ancient wisdom of the Vedas and Upanishads, I acknowledge and honor those who have been integral to my journey, bridging the wisdom of the ancients with the insights of the modern era.

1. The Gardeners of Insight: Sunita Krishnan and Kunal Kapoor

My heartfelt appreciation goes to Sunita Krishnan and Kunal Kapoor, whose constant support and love have been crucial in cultivating the foundation of this journey. Their encouragement is a living testament to the Vedic teaching of "Satyam vada, dharmam cara," urging us to embrace truth and righteousness.

2. The Spectrum of Guidance: Guru Devendra Deshpande

I am grateful to Guru Devendra Deshpande, a revered mentor whose guidance has infused my life with a spectrum of enlightenment. The wisdom of the Upanishads teaches us "Tat Tvam Asi," a reminder of our intrinsic unity with the cosmos, a principle he embodies and imparts.

3. A Father's Enduring Love and Wisdom: AR Rajagopala Krishnan

I extend my deepest gratitude to my guiding star, AR Rajagopala Krishnan, whose love, wisdom, and steadfast encouragement have been my constant support. His nurturing has been a beacon of the Vedic wisdom, emphasizing the pivotal role of paternal guidance and love in our lives.

4. The Tapestry of Teachers: Illuminators of Knowledge

To the countless teachers who have illuminated my path with knowledge and insight, I express my appreciation. Whether in the form of gurus, friends, or the wisdom found within the pages of books, their teachings have enriched my journey, reflecting the Vedic adage, "Guru Brahma, Guru Vishnu," signifying the divine essence within all mentors.

5. The Inner Compass: Guiding Light Within

Last but certainly not least, I acknowledge and thank my own inner guidance—the compass that continues to illuminate my way. This inner wisdom, reminiscent of the Upanishadic revelation "Aham Brahmasmi," reminds me of the divine spark within, responsible for the creation of this work.

In the grand tapestry of existence, it is through the threads of gratitude that we weave the fabric of our connections. As we draw inspiration from the wisdom of the past and embrace the innovations of the present, let our expressions of gratitude serve as a harmonious symphony—a tribute to the timeless teachings of the Vedas and Upanishads. Together, we continue to nurture the garden of inspiration, cultivating a vibrant and ever-blooming landscape for all seekers of knowledge and wisdom.

Part 6
Integration of Technology for Manifesting Dreams

In the preceding chapters of "Cultivating Your Dreams into Reality," we embarked on a transformative journey exploring the intricacies of harnessing willpower, pioneering thinking, inner harmony through meditation and empowerments, specialized techniques, and living creatively. We delved into the depths of human potential, uncovering the pathways to manifesting our dreams into tangible realities. Now, as we culminate our exploration, we embark on a quest to integrate the latest technological advancements seamlessly into our pursuit of realizing our deepest aspirations.

In this chapter, we'll explore how cutting-edge technologies, tools, and practices can amplify our ability to manifest dreams and empower us to navigate the complexities of the modern world with greater clarity, efficiency, and creativity.

1. **Virtual Reality (VR) Visualization**: Imagine stepping into a virtual realm where your dreams come to life with vivid detail and immersive experiences. Virtual reality technology enables us to create virtual environments tailored to our desires, allowing us to visualize our goals with unparalleled realism. By immersing ourselves in these virtual landscapes, we can strengthen our mental imagery, reinforce positive beliefs, and cultivate unwavering confidence in our ability to manifest our dreams.

2. **Augmented Reality (AR) Empowerments**: Augmented reality overlays digital content onto the physical world, offering a unique platform for reinforcing empowerments and positive mantras. Through AR-enabled devices such as smartphones or smart glasses, we can surround ourselves with uplifting messages, empowering visuals, and empowerments aligned with our aspirations. By integrating AR into our daily lives, we infuse our physical environment with positivity, motivation, and reminders of our inherent potential.

3. **Mind-Machine Interface (MMI) Meditation**: Mind-machine interface technology facilitates direct communication between the brain and external devices, opening new frontiers in meditation and inner harmony. By leveraging EEG headsets or neurofeedback devices, we can monitor and modulate our brainwave activity in real-time, guiding our minds into states of deep relaxation, focus, and transcendence. MMI meditation empowers us to cultivate profound states of inner peace, clarity, and alignment, laying the foundation for manifesting our dreams from a place of centeredness and serenity.

4. **Artificial Intelligence (AI) Personalization**: Harnessing the power of artificial intelligence, we can personalize our manifestation journey to suit our unique preferences, strengths, and growth areas. AI algorithms analyze vast datasets related to our habits, behaviors, and aspirations, providing personalized insights, recommendations, and strategies for achieving our dreams. Whether it's optimizing our daily routines, refining our goal-setting techniques, or

offering tailored guidance on overcoming obstacles, AI becomes an indispensable ally in our quest for self-actualization.

These technological advancements represent just a glimpse of the myriad possibilities for integrating technology into our journey of manifesting dreams into reality. As we embrace these tools with intention, mindfulness, and discernment, we expand our capacity to create, innovate, and transform our lives in alignment with our highest visions.

In the following pages, we'll delve deeper into each of these technologies, exploring practical strategies, exercises, and applications to integrate them seamlessly into our daily practices. Through hands-on experimentation and open-minded exploration, we'll unlock the full potential of technology as a catalyst for realizing our wildest dreams.

Virtual Reality (VR) Visualization

Virtual reality (VR) has emerged as a revolutionary tool for transforming the way we perceive and interact with our dreams. By immersing ourselves in virtual environments tailored to our aspirations, we can enhance our visualization practices and accelerate the manifestation process. Here's how you can leverage VR visualization to amplify your journey towards realizing your dreams:

Setting the Scene: Begin by identifying a specific goal or dream that you wish to manifest. Whether it's advancing in your career, cultivating deeper relationships, or achieving personal growth milestones, clarity is key. Once you've defined your objective, envision the ideal scenario associated with its fulfillment. Picture yourself immersed in a virtual environment that vividly portrays the realization of your dream, complete with sights, sounds, and sensations that evoke a profound sense of achievement and fulfillment.

Immersive Visualization: Put on your VR headset and enter the virtual realm you've created. Allow yourself to fully immerse in the experience, engaging all your senses to amplify the realism of your visualization. Notice the details of your surroundings, the people you encounter, and the emotions that arise as you navigate through your dream scenario. By engaging in immersive visualization, you activate the neural pathways associated with your desired outcome, reinforcing positive beliefs and paving the way for its manifestation in the physical world.

Interactive Exploration: Take advantage of VR's interactive capabilities to actively engage with your dream environment. Interact with virtual objects, engage in simulated activities, and experiment with different scenarios to explore the nuances of your desired outcome. By actively participating in the virtual experience, you deepen your emotional connection to your dream, strengthening your resolve and commitment to its realization.

Affirmation Integration: Incorporate empowerments and positive mantras into your VR visualization practice to amplify its effectiveness. As you navigate through your virtual environment, repeat empowering empowerments related to your goal with conviction and sincerity. Allow the immersive nature of VR to heighten the impact of your empowerments, anchoring them deeply into your subconscious mind and aligning your thoughts and actions with your desired outcome.

Reflective Integration: Upon exiting the virtual realm, take time to reflect on your experience and insights gained during the visualization process. Journal about any notable observations, breakthroughs, or shifts in perspective that occurred during your VR session. Use this reflection as an opportunity to refine your vision, adjust your approach, and reaffirm your commitment to manifesting your dreams.

Incorporating VR visualization into your manifestation practice offers a powerful means of amplifying your creative potential, enhancing your visualization skills, and accelerating the realization of your dreams. As you embrace this innovative technology with intention and dedication, you unlock new dimensions of possibility and propel yourself towards the fulfillment of your deepest aspirations.

Mind-Machine Interface (MMI) Meditation

As we delve deeper into the integration of technology with our journey of manifesting dreams into reality, we encounter the transformative potential of mind-machine interface (MMI) meditation. MMI technology facilitates direct communication between the brain and external devices, offering a revolutionary approach to enhancing meditation practices and cultivating inner harmony. Here's how you can harness MMI meditation to amplify your manifestation journey:

Understanding MMI Technology: MMI devices, such as EEG headsets or neurofeedback systems, utilize sensors to detect and measure brainwave activity in real-time. These devices translate neural signals into actionable data, enabling users to monitor and modulate their mental states with unprecedented precision and control. By interfacing with the brain's electrical activity, MMI technology provides insights into our cognitive processes and offers a pathway to optimize our mental well-being.

Setting the Stage: Find a quiet and comfortable space where you can engage in meditation without distractions. Put on your MMI device and ensure it is properly calibrated to accurately capture your brainwave activity. Take a few moments to center yourself and cultivate a state of relaxation and receptivity before beginning your meditation practice.

Neurofeedback Meditation: Start your meditation session by focusing on your breath and allowing your mind to settle into a state of calm awareness. As you breathe deeply and rhythmically, observe any fluctuations in your mental state and corresponding changes in your brainwave patterns displayed on the MMI device. Use this real-time feedback to guide your meditation, adjusting your focus and techniques to optimize your brainwave activity for deep relaxation, heightened concentration, or transcendent states of consciousness.

Visualization Enhancement: Integrate visualization techniques into your MMI meditation practice to amplify its effectiveness. As you enter a state of relaxed awareness, visualize yourself immersed in a serene and tranquil environment conducive to meditation, such as a peaceful garden or tranquil beach. Use the feedback from your MMI device to enhance your visualization experience, synchronizing your mental imagery with the desired brainwave patterns associated with deep states of meditation and inner harmony.

Affirmation Reinforcement: Incorporate empowerments and positive mantras into your MMI meditation practice to reinforce your intentions and cultivate a mindset of abundance and empowerment. As you meditate, repeat empowerments aligned with your goals and aspirations, infusing them with the power of your focused attention and heightened brainwave coherence. Use the feedback from your MMI device to reinforce the neural pathways associated with your empowerments, anchoring them deeply into your subconscious mind and facilitating their manifestation into reality.

Reflection and Integration: Conclude your MMI meditation session with a period of reflection and integration. Take note of any insights, revelations, or shifts in consciousness that occurred during your practice, and journal about your experience to deepen your understanding and insight. Use this reflective process to integrate the lessons learned from your MMI meditation into your daily life, applying them to overcome challenges, cultivate inner peace, and manifest your dreams with clarity and conviction.

Incorporating MMI meditation into your manifestation journey offers a revolutionary approach to enhancing your mental well-being, optimizing your meditation practices, and accelerating your progress towards realizing your dreams. As you embrace this cutting-edge technology with mindfulness and intention, you unlock new dimensions of inner harmony, creativity, and transformation, paving the way for a life of profound fulfillment and purpose.

Artificial Intelligence (AI) Personalization

As we continue our exploration of integrating cutting-edge technology with the timeless wisdom of manifesting dreams into reality, we encounter the transformative potential of artificial intelligence (AI) personalization. AI algorithms analyze vast datasets related to our habits, behaviors, and aspirations, providing personalized insights, recommendations, and strategies for achieving our dreams. Here's how you can harness AI personalization to amplify your manifestation journey:

Understanding AI Personalization: AI personalization encompasses a range of technologies and techniques that leverage machine learning algorithms to tailor experiences, content, and recommendations to individual preferences and characteristics. From personalized recommendations on streaming platforms to customized fitness routines generated by health apps, AI personalization is ubiquitous in our daily lives. By harnessing the power of AI, we can access personalized insights and guidance to optimize our manifestation practices and accelerate our progress towards realizing our dreams.

Data Collection and Analysis: Begin by collecting data related to your habits, behaviors, and aspirations using digital tools and platforms. This data may include information about your daily routines, goals, preferences, strengths, and growth areas. Use AI-powered analytics tools to analyze this data and uncover patterns, trends, and correlations that provide valuable insights into your manifestation journey. By gaining a deeper understanding of your unique characteristics and tendencies, you can identify areas for growth and optimization, paving the way for more effective manifestation strategies.

Personalized Recommendations: Once you have gathered and analyzed your data, leverage AI-powered recommendation engines to receive personalized insights and recommendations tailored to your specific needs and goals. Whether it's personalized goal-setting frameworks, customized visualization exercises, or targeted empowerments, AI algorithms can provide recommendations based on your individual preferences and characteristics. Use these recommendations to refine your manifestation practices, optimize your approach, and align your actions with your highest aspirations.

Adaptive Learning: Embrace AI-powered adaptive learning technologies to continuously optimize your manifestation journey based on real-time feedback and insights. Adaptive learning algorithms analyze your interactions, progress, and outcomes to dynamically adjust and personalize your experiences over time. By incorporating adaptive learning principles into your manifestation practices, you can adapt to changing circumstances, overcome obstacles, and maximize your growth and development with unparalleled precision and efficiency.

Integration with Daily Life: Integrate AI personalization seamlessly into your daily life to enhance your manifestation journey and support your ongoing growth and development. Whether it's leveraging AI-powered productivity tools to optimize your workflow, using personalized wellness apps to support your physical and mental well-being, or accessing tailored content and resources to inspire and motivate you, AI personalization becomes an invaluable ally in your quest to manifest your dreams into reality.

Reflection and Iteration: As you leverage AI personalization to enhance your manifestation journey, take time to reflect on your experiences and outcomes. Evaluate the effectiveness of the personalized recommendations and strategies you have implemented, and iterate based on the insights gained. Use this reflective process to refine your approach, experiment with new techniques, and continue evolving towards the realization of your dreams with clarity, intention, and purpose.

Incorporating AI personalization into your manifestation journey offers a dynamic and adaptive approach to optimizing your practices, harnessing your strengths, and overcoming challenges on the path to realizing your dreams. By embracing the latest advancements in AI technology with openness and curiosity, you unlock new possibilities for growth, transformation, and self-discovery, propelling yourself towards a future of boundless potential and fulfillment.

Living Mindfully: Embodying the Synthesis

As we synthesize the wisdom gleaned from the preceding chapters of "Cultivating Your Dreams into Reality" and integrate the latest technological advancements, we arrive at the nexus of mindful living – a harmonious fusion of willpower, pioneering thinking, inner harmony, specialized techniques, and creative manifestation. In this chapter, we delve into the practice of living mindfully, embodying the synthesis of ancient wisdom and modern innovation to manifest our dreams into tangible reality.

Cultivating Awareness: Begin by cultivating awareness of your thoughts, emotions, and actions in each moment. Practice mindfulness meditation to observe the fluctuations of your mind without judgment or attachment. By cultivating present-moment awareness, you develop the clarity and discernment necessary to align your thoughts and actions with your deepest aspirations.

Harnessing Willpower: Utilize the power of willpower to set clear intentions and pursue your dreams with unwavering determination. Draw upon the techniques discussed in Part 1 to strengthen your resolve, overcome obstacles, and stay committed to your vision, even in the face of adversity. By harnessing the force of willpower, you propel yourself towards the realization of your highest potential.

Engaging Pioneering Thinking: Embrace pioneering thinking as a catalyst for innovation and creative problem-solving.

Cultivate a mindset of curiosity, experimentation, and adaptability, as discussed in Part 2, to explore new possibilities and transcend perceived limitations. By challenging conventional thinking patterns and embracing a spirit of exploration, you expand your horizons and uncover novel pathways towards manifesting your dreams.

Nurturing Inner Harmony: Deepen your practice of meditation and empowerments, as explored in Part 3, to nurture inner harmony and cultivate a sense of peace and alignment within yourself. Engage in regular meditation sessions to quiet the chatter of the mind and connect with the stillness at the core of your being. Use empowerments to reinforce positive beliefs and cultivate a mindset of abundance and empowerment.

Applying Special Techniques: Explore specialized techniques and tools, as discussed in Part 4, to optimize your manifestation practices and accelerate your progress towards your goals. Whether it's leveraging virtual reality visualization, mind-machine interface meditation, or artificial intelligence personalization, integrate the latest technological advancements with intention and mindfulness to amplify your manifestation journey.

Living Creatively: Embrace the practice of living creatively, as explored in Part 5, to manifest the divine within and unleash your innate creative potential. Cultivate a sense of wonder and awe towards the world around you, seeing every moment as an opportunity for expression and exploration. Allow your creativity to flow freely, uninhibited by self-doubt or fear, as you co-create your reality with the universe.

Synthesizing Wisdom and Innovation: Finally, embrace the synthesis of ancient wisdom and modern innovation as you navigate the journey of manifesting your dreams into reality. Honor the timeless principles of willpower, pioneering thinking, inner harmony, and creative expression, while embracing the latest technological tools and practices to support your growth and evolution.

Reflection and Integration: Take time to reflect on your journey thus far and integrate the insights gained from each chapter into your daily life. Cultivate a sense of gratitude for the progress you've made and the lessons learned along the way. Use this reflective process to refine your approach, deepen your understanding, and continue evolving towards the manifestation of your highest dreams and aspirations.

Embracing Holistic Integration: The Synergy of Tradition and Innovation

In our quest to manifest our dreams into reality, we have journeyed through the tapestry of willpower, pioneering thinking, inner harmony, specialized techniques, and creative living. Each chapter has provided valuable insights and practical tools to guide us along the path of self-discovery and transformation. Now, as we stand at the threshold of culmination, we find ourselves poised to embrace holistic integration – the synergy of tradition and innovation.

Honoring Ancient Wisdom: At the core of our journey lies a profound reverence for ancient wisdom – the timeless teachings and principles that have guided humanity for millennia. From the Stoic philosophy of willpower to the Eastern practices of meditation and affirmation, we draw inspiration from diverse traditions that illuminate the path to self-realization and fulfillment. By honoring these timeless truths, we anchor ourselves in a rich tapestry of wisdom that transcends cultural boundaries and speaks to the universal aspirations of the human spirit.

Embracing Modern Innovation: In tandem with ancient wisdom, we embrace the cutting-edge innovations and technologies that define the modern era. From virtual reality visualization to artificial intelligence personalization, we harness the power of innovation to amplify our manifestation practices and accelerate our progress towards our goals. By embracing the latest tools and techniques, we tap into the limitless potential of human ingenuity and creativity, forging new pathways to realizing our dreams in the digital age.

Creating Synergy: As we integrate tradition and innovation, we create a synergistic fusion that harnesses the best of both worlds. We draw upon ancient wisdom to cultivate inner resilience, clarity, and purpose, while leveraging modern technology to enhance our visualization, affirmation, and meditation practices. Through this harmonious integration, we unlock new levels of effectiveness and efficiency in our manifestation journey, bridging the gap between the timeless truths of the past and the limitless possibilities of the future.

Cultivating Balance: Central to holistic integration is the cultivation of balance – a dynamic equilibrium that honors the interplay of tradition and innovation, ancient wisdom and modern technology. We recognize that true mastery lies not in rigid adherence to the past or blind pursuit of the future, but in the ability to navigate the ever-changing landscape of life with grace and wisdom. By cultivating balance in our approach to manifestation, we harmonize our inner and outer worlds, aligning with the natural rhythms of existence and unfolding our potential with ease and grace.

Fostering Evolution: Finally, holistic integration fosters evolution – a continuous process of growth, adaptation, and transformation. We embrace change as an inherent aspect of life, welcoming new insights, experiences, and opportunities with open arms. As we evolve, both individually and collectively, we expand our capacity to manifest our dreams into reality, co-creating a world that reflects the highest aspirations of humanity.

Harmonizing Tradition and Innovation: A Roadmap for Manifestation Mastery

As we approach the culmination of our journey in "Cultivating Your Dreams into Reality," we find ourselves at a crossroads of tradition and innovation, ancient wisdom and modern technology. In this chapter, we provide a comprehensive roadmap for manifestation mastery that harmonizes the timeless principles explored in the preceding chapters with the latest advancements in technology and practice.

1. **Setting Clear Intentions:** Begin by setting clear intentions for your manifestation journey. Draw upon the power of willpower, as discussed in Part 1, to cultivate unwavering determination and focus. Clearly define your goals and aspirations, anchoring them in a vision that resonates deeply with your heart and soul.

2. **Cultivating Pioneering Thinking:** Embrace pioneering thinking as a guiding principle in your manifestation practice. Challenge conventional thinking patterns and explore new possibilities with an open mind and creative spirit. Use the art of pioneering thinking, as discussed in Part 2, to innovate and adapt your approach to manifestation in alignment with your evolving vision.

3. **Nurturing Inner Harmony:** Prioritize inner harmony as the foundation of your manifestation journey. Engage in regular meditation and affirmation practices, as explored in Part 3, to cultivate a sense of peace, clarity, and alignment within yourself. Use these practices to quiet the chatter of the mind and connect with the wisdom of your inner guidance.

4. **Applying Special Techniques:** Explore specialized techniques and tools to optimize your manifestation practices. Leverage the latest advancements in technology, such as virtual reality visualization and artificial intelligence personalization, to amplify your visualization, affirmation, and meditation practices. Experiment with different techniques to discover what resonates most deeply with you.

5. **Living Creatively:** Embrace a mindset of creative living as you navigate the manifestation journey. Tap into your innate creativity and imagination to co-create your reality with the universe. Use creative expression as a means of channeling your intentions into tangible form, as discussed in Part 5, and infuse your daily life with passion, purpose, and joy.

6. **Embodying Holistic Integration:** Finally, embody holistic integration as the guiding principle of your manifestation mastery. Harmonize the timeless wisdom of ancient traditions with the latest innovations in technology and practice. Strive for balance and alignment in all aspects of your life, honoring the interconnectedness of mind, body, and spirit.

Embracing the Journey: Manifestation as a Way of Life

As we conclude our exploration of "Cultivating Your Dreams into Reality," we recognize that manifestation is not merely a destination to be reached but a way of life to be embraced. In this final chapter, we reflect on the key principles and practices discussed throughout the book and offer guidance on how to integrate them into your daily life, making manifestation a continuous and transformative journey.

1. **Cultivating Gratitude:** Begin each day with a heart full of gratitude for the blessings in your life. Take a moment to express appreciation for the opportunities, experiences, and relationships that enrich your journey. Gratitude opens the door to abundance and invites more blessings to flow into your life.

2. **Practicing Mindfulness:** Embrace mindfulness as a cornerstone of your manifestation practice. Cultivate present-moment awareness in all aspects of your life, from mundane tasks to profound moments of insight. By staying grounded in the present, you align with the creative power of the universe and manifest your intentions with greater clarity and precision.

3. **Setting Daily Intentions:** Start each day with a clear intention for what you wish to manifest. Write down your intentions and empowerments, anchoring them in your consciousness and setting the stage for their realization. By aligning your thoughts, words, and actions with your intentions, you harness the power of focused intentionality to manifest your dreams.

4. **Engaging in Self-Reflection:** Take time for regular self-reflection to assess your progress, celebrate your successes, and learn from your challenges. Journaling, meditation, or quiet contemplation can provide valuable insights into your inner landscape and guide your next steps on the path of manifestation.

5. **Cultivating Resilience:** Embrace challenges and setbacks as opportunities for growth and transformation. Cultivate resilience in the face of adversity, drawing upon the inner

strength and determination discussed in Part 1. Trust in your ability to overcome obstacles and navigate the twists and turns of life's journey with grace and resilience.

6. **Connecting with Others:** Nurture meaningful connections with others who support and inspire your manifestation journey. Surround yourself with like-minded individuals who share your vision and values, and collaborate with them to co-create a reality aligned with your highest aspirations. Together, you amplify each other's intentions and accelerate the manifestation process.

7. **Celebrating Milestones:** Celebrate your achievements and milestones along the way, no matter how small they may seem. Recognize and acknowledge the progress you've made, and take time to savor the joy and fulfillment that comes with manifesting your dreams into reality. Celebrating your successes reinforces positive momentum and fuels your continued progress on the journey.

As you embrace manifestation as a way of life, remember that the journey is as important as the destination. Stay open to the magic and mystery of the universe, and trust that the seeds you plant will blossom in divine timing. Manifestation is not about controlling outcomes but about aligning with the flow of life and co-creating with the infinite intelligence that guides us all. Embrace the journey with an open heart and mind, and watch as your dreams unfold before your eyes.

Wishing You Good Luck and Persistence

As we come to the end of our journey through "Cultivating Your Dreams into Reality," I want to extend my heartfelt congratulations to you. You have embarked on a profound exploration of self-discovery, transformation, and manifestation, and I commend you for your dedication and commitment to realizing your dreams.

Throughout this book, we have delved into the depths of willpower, pioneering thinking, inner harmony, specialized techniques, and creative living. We have explored ancient wisdom and modern innovation, synthesizing the timeless principles of manifestation with the latest advancements in technology and practice.

Now, as you stand at the threshold of your manifestation journey, I offer you these final words of encouragement:

Good Luck: May luck be on your side as you continue on your path of manifestation. May serendipitous encounters, unexpected opportunities, and fortunate events align with your intentions and propel you towards the realization of your dreams. Trust in the benevolent forces of the universe and know that everything happens for a reason, even if it may not always be immediately apparent.

Persistence: Remember that persistence is the key to manifestation mastery. Stay steadfast in your commitment to your goals and aspirations, even in the face of challenges and setbacks. Cultivate resilience, determination, and unwavering faith in your ability to manifest your dreams into reality. Know that every step you take, no matter how small, brings you closer to your desired outcome.

As you move forward on your manifestation journey, carry with you the wisdom you have gained from this book and the tools and techniques you have acquired along the way. Trust in the power of your intentions, the guidance of your inner wisdom, and the support of the universe to guide you towards the fulfillment of your deepest desires.

With a heart full of hope, a mind filled with possibility, and a spirit imbued with resilience, may you continue to manifest your dreams into reality with grace and ease. May your journey be filled with joy, fulfillment, and abundance in all areas of your life.

Wishing you good luck and persistence on your journey of manifestation mastery.

With warm regards, **Vinay Rajagopal Iyer**

Recommended resources

Here are some recommended resources that cover various aspects of manifestation, willpower, pioneering thinking, inner harmony, special techniques, and creative living:

1. Manifestation and Law of Attraction:
   - "The Secret of the Nagas" by Amish Tripathi (fictional but carries philosophical aspects)
   - "The Secret" by Rhonda Byrne
   - "Ask and It Is Given: Learning to Manifest Your Desires" by Esther and Jerry Hicks
   - "The Power of Your Subconscious Mind" by Joseph Murphy
   - "You Can Heal Your Life" by Louise Hay
   - "The Magic of Thinking Big" by David J. Schwartz
2. Willpower and Self-Discipline:
   - "The Monk Who Sold His Ferrari" by Robin Sharma
   - "The 5 AM Club: Own Your Morning, Elevate Your Life" by Robin Sharma
   - "The Power of Positive Thinking" by Norman Vincent Peale

- "The Willpower Instinct: How Self-Control Works, Why It Matters, and What You Can Do to Get More of It" by Kelly McGonigal
- "Atomic Habits: An Easy & Proven Way to Build Good Habits & Break Bad Ones" by James Clear
- "Mindset: The New Psychology of Success" by Carol S. Dweck
- "Grit: The Power of Passion and Perseverance" by Angela Duckworth
- "Deep Work: Rules for Focused Success in a Distracted World" by Cal Newport

3. Pioneering Thinking and Creativity:

   - "Stay Hungry Stay Foolish" by Rashmi Bansal
   - "Think with Me: Fundamentals for Entrepreneurial Success" by Subrata Roy
   - "Wings of Fire" by Dr. A.P.J. Abdul Kalam
   - "Think and Grow Rich" by Napoleon Hill
   - "Big Magic: Creative Living Beyond Fear" by Elizabeth Gilbert
   - "The Artist's Way: A Spiritual Path to Higher Creativity" by Julia Cameron
   - "Originals: How Non-Conformists Move the World" by Adam Grant
   - "The War of Art: Break Through the Blocks and Win Your Inner Creative Battles" by Steven Pressfield

4. Inner Harmony and Meditation:
    - "Autobiography of a Yogi" by Paramahansa Yogananda
    - "Mindfulness: Finding Peace in a Frantic World" by Dr. Kabir Sattar
    - "Ashtavakra Gita" translated by Swami Sarvapriyananda
    - "The Power of Now: A Guide to Spiritual Enlightenment" by Eckhart Tolle
    - "Wherever You Go, There You Are: Mindfulness Meditation in Everyday Life" by Jon Kabat-Zinn
    - "The Miracle of Mindfulness: An Introduction to the Practice of Meditation" by Thich Nhat Hanh
    - "Meditation for Beginners" by Jack Kornfield
    - "The Headspace Guide to Meditation and Mindfulness: How Mindfulness Can Change Your Life in Ten Minutes a Day" by Andy Puddicombe

5. Special Techniques and Advanced Practices:
    - "The Seven Spiritual Laws of Success" by Deepak Chopra
    - "Inner Engineering: A Yogi's Guide to Joy" by Sadhguru
    - "Awakening Inner Guru: A Revolutionary Path to Freedom, Happiness, and Fulfillment" by Dr. Neeraj Kumar
    - "Breaking the Habit of Being Yourself: How to Lose Your Mind and Create a New One" by Dr. Joe Dispenza

- "The Biology of Belief: Unleashing the Power of Consciousness, Matter & Miracles" by Bruce H. Lipton
- "Becoming Supernatural: How Common People Are Doing the Uncommon" by Dr. Joe Dispenza
- "Super Brain: Unleashing the Explosive Power of Your Mind to Maximize Health, Happiness, and Spiritual Well-Being" by Deepak Chopra and Rudolph E. Tanzi
- "The Power of Intention: Learning to Co-create Your World Your Way" by Dr. Wayne W. Dyer

These resources encompass a wide range of topics related to personal growth, manifestation, and spiritual development, providing valuable insights and practical techniques to support you on your journey of cultivating your dreams into reality.

www.ingramcontent.com/pod-product-compliance
Lightning Source LLC
LaVergne TN
LVHW061546070526
838199LV00077B/6916